EDUCATION AMONG SCHEDULED CASTES

Education among Scheduled Castes

Privatization and Enrolment Perspectives in Higher Education

Dharma Rakshit Gautam

SHIPRA

Rs. 850

ISBN: 978-81-7541-654-3

First Published in India in 2012

Education Among Scheduled Caste: Privatization and Enrolment Perspectives in Higher Education

Published by:

SHIPRA PUBLICATIONS
LG 18-19, Pankaj Central Market,
I.P. Ext., Patparganj, Delhi 110092, India
Ph.: 011- 2223 5152, 2223 6152
Email: info@shiprapublication.com

Preface

Higher education is related to skill oriented learning that holds potential to make economic as well as social advancement in the contemporary world. It could therefore act as a potent tool to further development process in a state and also sustain the challenges posed by the current wave of globalization. Importance with which higher education is well associated makes it essential to be universally available in a state. In other words the responsibility lies over the state to expand higher education system such that it may match the demographic increase. India with a large younger population has a unique position with a surplus human resource that could be well utilized when given higher education. The predicament then is about the mechanism through which expansion of higher education could be sought. Option could be between public and private way of doing it. However there are certain pros and cons related to each of these and should therefore be selected wisely according to the prevailing socio-economic scenario in the state. Economic liberalization induced by the present globalization ushered trend of privatization of higher education. There is no denial to the fact that such a trend has major social and also economic (in long run) implications for a state.

Indian social structure is of peculiar nature where some sections of society have perennially been discriminated and were left untouched from any mechanism ensuring enlightenment. Scheduled caste is one such category. Their subjugated positions were recognized in the modern colonial period and after independence were granted reservation (to ensure equality of opportunity) in the constitution. Social normative structure didn't however make serious attention to it delaying the process further. And very lately some affirmative legal measures did mark rudimentary beginning for their enrolment in education albeit drop out rate is still high thanks to their socially discriminated and therefore disadvantaged position. This could be witnessed while going through available educational data which makes their absence conspicuous vis-à-vis other communities of Indian society. Here it can be noted that no claim for the satisfactory educational enrolment of other sections is made but comparative subjugation of the referred group can't be denied. Their low enrolment in higher education could be seen as one of the outcome of their hitherto miserable education position. Moreover, their opportunity cost of getting higher education also got enhanced with the coming of globalization.

In this scenario, inevitable is the state's protection to ensure enrolment of scheduled caste students in higher education. However, recent attempt by Indian state government to open higher education to private (state and non state) players could jeopardize the interests of these students in particular and other economically deprived students at large. This may transform 'right' to get higher education into a 'struggle' between haves and have-nots where right of the former would be acknowledged. And in this struggle scheduled caste students would suffer the most as their claim would be the lowest accruing to their condition as of economically as well as socially poor.

Present work holds this opinion and therefore tries to analyze the current modification in terms of privatization (in Indian higher education) and what implication it would be drawing on marginalized sections like that of scheduled castes. While making such analysis various educational policies pertaining to higher education in India have been discussed. Further an attempt is made to analyze the current trends of enrolment in higher education by scheduled castes which is then compared with the scenario of other students' enrolment during the same period (after privatization in 1991). The study like this is an attempt to have insight of the higher educational scenario of scheduled castes in the wake of privatization which could be utilized to formulate a fuller picture by doing necessary further research. The period of data collection through secondary sources is from 1191 to 2005 and therefore entire content to be seen with the same perspective. Though utmost care has been taken to present and discuss the available data from secondary sources still there could be some of the human error to which only I may be held responsible. I'd love to progress upon the lines suggested in your feedback and responses.

Dharma Rakshit Gautam

Acknowledgements

Through this space I'd like to thank several persons who made this work a possibility. The foremost name that comes to my memory in this regard is of Dr. Y. Josephine under whose guidance this study was conducted. Through her excellent guidance and motivation I was able to complete this study. The liberty with which access to different faculty members of my institution (NUEPA) was made contributed significantly to sail through smoothly in my endeavor. The scholarly advice and help coming via different research scholars of NUEPA and JNU did hold the importance to be mentioned here. Arvind, Santosh, Sudhir, Shiv, Kshipra, Sudhanshu, and Salma are some of these. Here mentioning the name of Sanghamitra is of unique significance who contributed heavily in terms of valuable critical notes. The list would be incomplete if I'd forget the support I got from the different personnel at the library of NUEPA, and JNU. It would be a gross mistake to miss the name of very important Mr. D. Kumar of Shipra publications whose personal interest and support made this book a reality. His meticulous editing helped me to present my work in a better fashion.

In all my way to fulfill this task my family had always shown immense faith in my abilities that acted as a source of inspiration to move ahead. Therefore it becomes essential to acknowledge their blind faith in me. Mummyji, Daddyji, Bhaiya, Bhabhiji, Gudia and little angel 'Samyak' have contributed in their own way to keep me going!

Lastly I'd like to thank in anticipation all the readers who may contribute in terms of their suggestions, comments and other forms of feedback while going through this book.

Contents

Abbreviations

A.P. : Andhra Pradesh
CABE : Central Advisory Board of Education
DU : Delhi University
GER : Gross Enrolment Ratio
H.P. : Himachal Pradesh
JNU : Jawaharlal Nehru University
MHRD : Ministry of Human Resource and Development
M.P. : Madhya Pradesh
M.Phil. : Master of Philosophy
N.C.T. : National Capital Territory
NUEPA : National University of Educational Planning and Administration
PG : Postgraduate
Ph.D. : Doctor of Philosophy
SC : Scheduled Caste
T.N. : Tamil Nadu
UG : Undergraduate
UGC : University Grants Commission
U.T. : Union Territory
U.K. : Uttarakhand
U.P. : Uttar Pradesh

List of Tables

List of Figures

1

Contextualizing Higher Education of Scheduled Castes in the Wake of Privatization

> "Higher education must lead the march back to the fundamentals of human relationships, to the old discovery that is ever new, that man does not live by bread alone".
>
> – *John A. Hannah*

The path of liberalization of all the sectors of Indian economy began in the last decade of 20th century. In the journey of almost twenty years, the concept has got wide acclamation and appreciation that it has transcended the core economic boundaries and has permeated in other social sector(s). There has been deliberate attempt (taking inspiration from the western industrial societies) to strike at bounteous social problems of the Indian society with desperate (not gradual) private (surmised economically efficient) players. It is, like, believing that economic development would lead to societal progress (without undoing the bondage with which different sections of Indian society are hierarchically tied). To everyone's surprise such a belief is cynical and fallacious as in a society which is stratified on hierarchical lines, economic benefits would not percolate down in a bottom up fashion channelizing major advantage to the lowest strata (who needs it most) rather it is other way round diverging the gap further.

With the argument for private players in education, it is quite obvious a stand that such a proposal is more democratic. However it is worthwhile to note that it may strengthen inequality (economic as well as social) in society and would not lead to social integration in the State. India has a uniform social set up with conspicuous feature of caste based rigidities and inequalities. Such a division of (hierarchical) society (on primordial lines) has a unilateral and enforcing relation at the economic horizon. However, it (economic horizon) was needed to be made independent of social ascriptions together with a symbiotic relationship with social structures making social mobility possible and dynamic.

Making provisions for liberalization and henceforth privatization of education in general or that of higher education particularly would imply the State's support for hitherto existing status quo in the society. In other words, the State (in this way) is moving back from Modern welfarist principle to pre- modern level in the name of having an economic viable option. This could be said as it is witnessed that in India access to productive resources as education is governed by social inequality, i.e. 'Caste'. And thus, children from lower castes are more educationally (henceforth economically) disadvantaged vis-à-vis upper caste children (Desai & Dubey, 2011).

Thus despite several constitutional provisions acting as an obligation for the State, lower caste people especially the scheduled castes have remained socially excluded[1] . Their exclusion becomes critical and more or less immutable[2] when they are made devoid of control of productive resources as land or from the mechanism to have better economic control and life chances, that is 'education'.

The present century is marked by high technological and industrial revolution driven by the knowledge based socio-economic set up. In such a scenario, every state is competing with other(s) to have a better survival and is attempting to have a bigger *'flow'* of knowledge-based society strengthening the *'stock'* of wealth in varied forms indicating the 'development' status of the state. In this regard, it can be noted that a knowledge-based social set up has a symbiotic relationship with higher education, education which equips a man with skills to enhance the capabilities[3] . There is no doubt about the fact that both the elementary and secondary education act as a basis for higher education and yields immediate returns and benefit. At the same time higher education has its own distinct place and importance, making a way for assured long-term benefits essentially required by a state to be judged high on the parameters reflecting development. Having a glance over the importance attached with the higher education, it seems appropriate to categorize such education into the nomenclature of *'Merit'* Good or Service (at least Merit II Good, Tilak, 2004). Though this term was coined and used by *Musgrave* in 1959[4], its relevance is true hitherto.

Merit goods are those which if driven by the traditional notion of consumer sovereignty, will be under supplied or under consumed. Therefore, such goods need State's control to make maximum welfare among its people. When left with consumers in case of these goods, there's possibility of preference for short run private benefits at the cost of larger individual as well as social benefits it would be deriving at longer period of time. Here vital becomes the prior 'information' relating to the benefits accruing to consumption of such goods. 'Lack of information' or 'myopic vision' may lead to lag in enrollment in education; a measure for human as well as social development of a State.

In order to assign importance to a good, social as well as spatial incidence of such good needs to be ascertained. It is to be decided which communities are deriving benefit with consumption of such good, higher education in our case, and what is the extent of their location, i.e. local, regional or national.

The issue of getting 'returns' (benefits) from higher education as a private affair is posed as appropriate justification to discard higher education from 'Merit' good category. However, such a generalization stands far from reality in the case of hierarchically stratified society like India. In Indian social system, neither there is universal and equal benefits across different segments and sections (particularly 'caste') nor is the information about externalities of higher education is spelled among existing stratifications. There can't be complete denial to have an argument about ineffective supply of higher education for the scheduled caste students to match it with the demands or expectations from the market. But such a discussion at this juncture would remain outside the scope of the present piece of writing.

In the wake of existing hierarchies, the concept of 'social capital' could not have lived its purpose as there's lack of investment to other segments' potential. The result is hierarchical perception or imperfect knowledge of the benefits to be derived from higher education where those at the higher level may perceive it more and could readily invest in it. But those lying at the lowest pedestal, for example scheduled castes could not foresee the future benefits of higher education and may rather evade such burden (involving costs). It happens so for the reason that 'advantages of education are more evident to the informed than the uninformed'[5].

Also, it's noteworthy that its opportunity cost for these (in particular) with humble status is too much to attract them in short run. Higher education has gained significance in the present globalised world and therefore should be treated as 'Merit good' at least in the context of hitherto disadvantaged communities like scheduled castes. However the chance of contingent advantage is most probable that would further the (composite) growth. Thus, the State should take responsibility to undo their distressed position enhancing their capabilities through higher education. The interference and tutelage of State is indispensable not only to make education accessible after bridging the social barriers but also to ensure successful participation of students of SC community. Further, if viewed through the lenses of our constitutional makers, it becomes explicit that compensatory advantages are must and would not contradict in any sense rather support equality of opportunity.

There are various positive externalities attached with higher education yielding both public and private benefits. And in a free market economic set up, the likely possibility is of i its under production and under consumption. The need therefore, is to regard higher education as a public good or service or public good with large private benefits. This is truer for a 'developing' welfare state like India where majority of the population is still unaware about the returns they can avail after their higher education.

There is a basic requirement to understand the importance of higher education not only for economic development but also for social development as various social externalities are attached to it like improvement in health, reduction in population and poverty, and strengthening of democracy (Tilak, 2005). In the process to achieve such a development 'inclusiveness', which has now become a buzzword for attainment of real development, is a mandatory precondition, for which however an egalitarian society is essentially needed. It has been found by various social scientists that education holds the key to ensure equity in the society, and therefore "States' surveillance" is to be there to ensure 'Equality of Opportunity' in all the existing areas in the state. In the case of higher education in order to have such an ideal existing the requirement is to have subsidized education at this level. And if our area of concern is students belonging to scheduled caste community who were and are facing the brunt of social discrimination as well as economic deprivation, then the need for such an assertion becomes much more desperate.

In the present era of Globalization, importance of higher education has grown manifold creating a need for subsidizing higher education as it is a 'mixed good' yielding social as well as individual returns. It is the higher education that produces the intellectual capital and knowledge relevant to the society to lead it towards the better future, where it can compete globally through its indigenously built knowledge economy and intellectual culture (Singh, 2005). However, it does not imply at all that private higher education won't yield social benefits, but the basic causes of private expansion remain religion, social advantage, and absorption of the accelerated demand for higher education (Levy, 2008).

In the last decade of the 20th century, entire world has witnessed a paradigm shift in almost all sectors of economy. The change was heralded by the phenomenon of 'Globalization' which was though ever present since time immemorial; its intensity was much limited to have its incidence on the policies of a state. With this phenomenon, a mammoth wave, conducive to the market forces, has spread all over the world. India, remaining no exception to such a change, has altered its policies irrespective of any sector, to the tune of globalization, and as a result started policies of liberalization and privatization. Consequently, in higher education sector of India, the government had loosened its control and paved way for mushrooming of the private institutions keeping the welfare concept at the stake or at the perils of private owner whose objectives are basically determined by the profit share it will be deriving. Generally, it is thought that 'private' control in a state is a symbol of efficiency and growth towards developed status. Also, there is an argument among scholars that public institutions are yielding mediocre quality and unwanted politicization. But this can't be accepted in full spirit and also there is a possibility to supervise its direction and henceforth improvement in quality through various pressure groups (Singh, 2005). At the same time it is to note down that privatization which has its move derived from profit orientation can't be a true agent of distributive justice (Tilak, 1991). And it seems that state control of higher education takes the state towards an enhanced status as has been witnessed in most of the developed nations in the world. The Punnaya Committee (1992)[6] pointed out the fallacy in thinking that higher education is not primarily state funded in developed countries. The committee found that fees formed less than 14 per cent of total expenditure in Britain. Higher education is primarily a state responsibility even in a country like USA, which has a free market economy and follows an avowed ideology of privatization. According to Glen Johnson, the government directly supports 78 per cent of the total enrolment in public institutions in USA. All public institutions receive nearly 60 per cent of their funds from the government. The government extends indirect support to the remaining 22 per cent of the total enrolment in private institutions giving federal aid to the students.

However, though India is having third largest higher education system in the world after China and USA, irony is that it is still struggling on the basic issues as access, quality, etc. thanks to its voluminous size of population and various socio-economic disparities that exists here. Since independence, Indian higher education has witnessed a progressive shift in all terms. From 1947 to 2006-07, while the number of universities has increased from 20 to 369, the number of colleges from 500 has rose up to 18064 during the same period. Till 2009, there are 20 central universities, 222 state universities, 109 deemed universities (institutions of high standard), 13 institutions of national importance established through central legislation and 5 institutes established through state legislation. Also, there has been a spectacular growth in the number of students enrolled in these higher educational institutions. From a meager figure of 0.174 million in 1950, the growth in enrollment has taken the figure to 11.028 million in 2006-07. However such an enrollment doesn't provide any respite for our policy makers as it is abysmally low with respect to the huge population of our nation. It can be rightly mentioned here that in India, three alternative methods are used to estimate the extent of access to higher education namely Gross Enrolment Ratio (GER), Net Enrolment Ratio (NER), and Enrolment of Eligible Ratio (EER). The GER measure the access level by taking the ratio of persons in all age group enrolled in various programs to total population in age group of 18 to 23. The NER measures the level of enrolment for age specific groups namely those in age group of 18 to 23. While EER measure the level of enrolment of those who completed higher secondary level education. These three concepts looks the access to higher education from three major perspectives.

In India, the data relating to access to higher education is provided by three different agencies i.e. (1) Selected Education Statistics (SES), (2) National Sample Survey (NSS), and (3) Population Census. The SES underestimates enrolment rates due to under reporting of enrolment in unrecognized institutions and also due to non-reporting of enrolment data on annual basis by some of the state governments. The problem with NSS and also Census data is that it is collected from households and is likely to over estimate the student enrollment in colleges and, universities as it might include those who are doing diploma or training programs in unrecognized institutions also. Among all the three it seems that data provided by SES is much closer to the real picture and is therefore reliable. At present the enrollment is 9.72 (GER, SES) which has marginally increased from 7.85 in 2001.

Since time immemorial education in India has remained a private affair and was limited to the male gender of upper three castes in general and to the 'Brahmin' Varna of the social set up in particular. It is due to such a hierarchical set up that entire education sector in India portrays a picture of concentrated participation of elite caste or class as there's hardly any distinction between the two in India. And the Indian *'mass'* that come under the Varna of *'Shudras' and untouchables* were denied to have access to education. Only after intervention of Britain as a colonial power there began some glimmering rays of hope albeit in theory for the masses to have fruit of education which was forbidden till now. During the British period, higher education was promoted in India through various *'Minutes', 'Acts', and 'Dispatch'*. English higher education in India began with M. Elphinston's 'Minute' of 1823 which paved way for the establishment of schools for teaching English and the European sciences. Later in 1835, came famous Macaulay's Minute which reiterated for promotion of European languages and sciences in India, though of course ulterior motives were attached to such promotion whose discussion remains outside the scope of this book. In 1854, there was Charles Wood Dispatch which is described as Magna Carta of English education in India (Power, 1995). The 'Dispatch' had got the idea, of establishing universities in India on the model of London University. As a consequence there was proliferation of universities and colleges across India and by the time of Independence there were 18 universities and several colleges. However, due to typical socio-cultural set up, there was not much to achieve for masses and education remained confined to the elite sections.

After Independence, Constitution of India remained a guide to all future policies, with determination to break down the shackles confronting the educational emancipation of hitherto deprived masses and to strive towards establishment of socialist, secular and democratic republic (Preamble, Constitution of India). Developments in Indian higher education began with Radhakrishnan Commission in 1948 which has provided the base to the same by redefining its needs, aims and methods. Thereafter higher education became an essential part of various policies on education (1968, 1986, 1992) and of different committees and commissions highlighting the key importance attached with the same in relation to India's real development.

If we look at the development of higher education in India in the last six decades, it becomes quite emphatic that there has been shift from socialism to capitalism. In the development, decade of 1980 forms a demarcating boundary and year 1991 as a watershed year. From 1980s there began a wave of self-financing institutions to provide higher education. Its approval has been sanctioned in NPE'86 and POA'92. In 1990s there has been major change in set up to dispense higher education. It has been shifted towards privatization as an impact of globalization and also as result of political move to liberalize and privatize all the sectors of economy in the name of making it more efficient. The major issue was of funding such education, whether government or private players (as a commodity in the market) to have upper hand. The point of debate revolves around the nature and utility of higher education, is it a merit and public good? After a long swerving, it has now been agreed that higher education is at least a Merit II good and a quasi-public good (Tilak, 2004). Therefore, as various social externalities are attached to higher education, it seems quite mandatory for a state to have a control over it as a part of its welfare activities. However globalization has a different tune to it and as a commodity higher education has been included in the list of traded items paving way for private players at the global level to encroach into the remotest location to fulfill their varied goals as religious, profit, so on and forth. Dancing to the tune of globalization, ministry of finance's paper on government subsidies (1997) declared higher education as a 'non-merit good' leaving it to private bodies to provide requisite finances (Azad, 2004).

Also, the World Bank in its educational sector paper (1995) recommended—

(a) The shift of public funding from education for higher education to lower levels of education.

(b) The expansion of secondary and higher education through increased privatization.

However, the reasoning of the World Bank has been contradicted by its own Task Force (2000), according to which *"an important ingredient in public interest in higher education is its role in creating a meritocratic society that is able to secure the best political leaders and civil servants, doctors and teachers, lawyers and engineers, and business, and civic leaders"*. The Task Force also challenged the "notion that public investment in higher education is socially inequitable... This argument overlooks the fact that an educated and skilled stratum is indispensable to the social and economic development of modern society... In addition, higher education has acted as a powerful mechanism for upward mobility, allowing the talented to thrive irrespective of their social origin". Following the global developments, where economics of commodities (goods and services) has been dogmatically applied to economics of education, privatization has been introduced in higher education sector in India. Before delving into detail, lets understand the term privatization, its implication in higher education, its legal basis in India, and most importantly what will it mean to masses especially the socially as well as economically disadvantaged community that has been categorized as scheduled castes.

In the broadest sense privatization implies doing away with the public control in favour of private or selling of responsibility from public to private authority. For higher education, the term includes a range of activities that are taking place on campus. Privatization includes more of privately centered decision making, floundering of the centrally accepted academic norms, loss of faculty autonomy and developing private funding sources. All over the world, higher education is been provided either completely by the state authorities (as in socialist countries) or as a part of mixed system where both the public and private sectors are existing. However the nature of such partnership differs e.g. in countries like Japan, Philippines, Korea, etc. there exists mass private sector while in states like India, the majority is with state. At the same time there are countries like France, Spain, Thailand, etc. where private players are at minimal end. Apart from this Scandinavian countries have a system where both public and private sectors exist under state funding (Tilak, 1991).

If we plan to categorize types of privatization that may exist in reality then we may end up having several type of it. But actually these can be broadly categorized into four depending on the intensity on a scale from cent per cent to zero per cent i.e. from purely unaided to fully aided (Tilak, 1991). After this generalization, if we need to categorize private institutions into different types then three types are generally seen:

(a) Institution that receive grant from the government, but the management is done by private people.
(b) Institutes that charge fees and offer approved syllabus of the government through university structures.
(c) Institutes that are purely private commercial entities with their own products (own course structure, fees and content) with foreign collaboration or with franchise to market products in Indian market.

The last category of institutes that are becoming very popular among the elite and the neo-rich posed certain problems that need to be discussed by academics and policymakers in detail (Chalam, 2004). Analysis of privatization of higher education is mainly drawn from the perspective of economics discipline which makes us to think it as efficient, however the picture remains incomplete without adding socio-cultural dimensions in the analysis. It has to be accepted that all such disciplines are equally important, and in such a background it becomes essential to dissect the issue utilizing the tools that are given under the constitution of India, legal document behind every policy of the state. Looking at privatization of higher education from the perspective of constitutional vision forces us to basically examine it on two standpoints i.e.

(a) If privatization is permissible under the various Constitutional provisions, and

(b) Desirability of privatization in the context of welfare of Scheduled Caste students

Issue of Permissibility

Vision and aim of Indian constitution has been given in its preamble which is why called spirit and backbone of the former[7]. The preamble promises a commitment by the people of India to secure to all Indian citizens the laudable objectives of liberty, justice, equality and fraternity. On an insightful look towards these ideals, it appears liberty, justice, equality and fraternity are interlinked and absence of one can not lead to fulfillment of other(s) e.g. without equality of status, equality of opportunity is unattainable. Similarly providing social justice is a pre condition for economic justice. It is evident that the ideals of social and economic justice and equality of opportunity, forms an integral part of the constitutional vision. This is further confirmed by the guarantee of equality as a fundamental right under Article 14 of the constitution, and the desirable guidelines for policy making a expressed through the Directive Principles of State Policy[8] Also, the 42nd Amendment in the constitution made it conspicuous that main ideal of constitution is socialism, which emphasizes the state engineered measures for attaining social and economic justice. Having a glance over Fundamental Rights that are mentioned in Part III of the constitution, it becomes clear that private persons are having full right to establish and manage educational institutions under Article 19 (1) (g) of the Indian constitution, as they are necessarily carrying on an occupation of their choice (T.M.A.Pai v State of Karnataka, 2002 8ccc481). In the case of minority institutions, Article 30 (1) guarantees religious and linguistic minorities the right to establish and administer educational institutions of their choice. As far as permissible restrictions are concerned, Article 19 (6) allows the state to impose reasonable restrictions on the right guaranteed by Article19 (1) (g) in the interests of the general public. Article 30 (1) on the other hand looks at first sight to be an absolute right, a matter of very important consequence for the minority institutions. It is therefore clear that on the permissibility issue, the constitution is affirmative. Further, the private interests in funding higher education have been given mandate on the ground of limits of economic capacity of the state.

Article 41 of the constitution[9] makes a provision for private participation in higher education. Now the question arises, who will get benefit out of such a situation and will avail access to higher education. It has been declared by the Universal Declaration of Human Rights (UNDHR) that higher education shall be made equally accessible to all on the basis of merit (Article 26 of UNDHR). From such a declaration it can be inferred that higher education is a human right and every meritorious student should have access to it. Such a normative situation could not take place under the commercialized higher education which is a next corollary to unrestricted privatization. Taking the issue further to access of the disadvantaged community of 'scheduled caste', issue of merit, which itself is an ambiguous concept, is of secondary importance for which the state in its constitution has made several special clauses in fundamental rights (Article 15 (4), Article 16 (4)) and also in Directive Principles of State Policy[10].

Desirability of Privatization in Context of Welfare of Scheduled Caste Students

Proponents of surmised economic efficiency of higher education, who believe that privatization is the most appropriate way to make higher education economically self-sufficient and efficient as financial incidence would now be directly on the consumer (student) of such good or service (according to the concept of higher education as a private good), have suggested various options as education loans, educational vouchers, etc. to take care of economic disadvantage of students of the state. Such proponents could be criticized on both fronts i.e. on their suggested measures' applicability in developing nation like India, and also on their myopic intellect which prohibits their vision to distinguish between economic and social disadvantage if we reduce our discussion to focus 'Scheduled Caste students' in India. Basic assumptions behind private support for higher education is that there are solely private returns coming out of it, in support of which public money should not be dispensed. However this is a disguised assumption as various social externalities like inhibiting anti-social behavior, upholding principles of democracy, etc. which are difficult to estimate in terms of value (Chattopadhyay, 2007) and therefore the need is to understand the social merit of this good or service.

Also, it is a folly of the research scholars who delineate higher education as distinct from primary education, which is considered as 'good' with high social externalities (Majumdar, 1997, Kumar, 2004).

It is to note down that higher education should not be dealt in isolation as it has linkages and provides inputs to primary education and therefore public investment in higher education is required (Majumdar,1983)[11].

With the coming of privatization several measures have been suggested to enhance the financial independence with fewer incidences on economically deprived students. Some of the propounded measures are:

(a) *Deregulation of fees*: Various suggestions have come up for deregulating fee for higher education. Punnaya Committee (1992) suggested for enhancement of fees to partly recover the cost of education. National Knowledge Commission has recommended enhancement of fees to recover 20 per cent of expenditure on universities. Also, there was proposal to have differentiated fees, on the basis of location, fees paid in the previously attended institute by the student, etc. (Chattopadhyay, 2007). However all such measures would make institute to function more like a profit maximizing entity in producing output from the inputs utilized and is therefore not appropriate for academic institutions as values can not be assigned in such academic institutions (Majumdar, 1983).

(b) *Education loans*: As a part of private payment of fees by the student, scheme of education loan has come into vogue but due to various imperfections in capital market (Hillman,2003, Lleras,2005) and due to negative empirical results adding to the list of defaulters (Chattopadhyay, 2007) makes this option unviable.

(c) *Human Capital Contract*: It's a contract between capital market and student where former agrees to pay for the latter's education which has to be returned in the form of income from job by the latter. This seems to be an unattractive idea in a developing nation like India where uncertainty regarding job prevails (Majumdar, 1983).

(d) *Education Vouchers*: Distribution of vouchers to economically disadvantaged students to choose best of the institute is the main aim of such a scheme. This scheme may not be fit for higher education due to high cost is involved and also there are administration cost and leakages (Chattopadhyay, 2007).

Apart from all this, if we need to focus on Scheduled Caste students' higher education then economic tools as discussed above are not viable and also are not sufficient as social discrimination (which this community is suffering) can't be undone with merely some economic tools. Though the economic problem is one of the major aspect to look over as it affects enrollment of these students (Chitnis,1972) as seen in a study where post matric scholarships had positively affected enrollment, it is not sufficient as the major problem affecting their participation is stereotypical (which is negatively biased) attitude towards them. Such a situation has been perfectly documented by Dr. B.R. Ambedkar as:

> "The problem of raising the lower order is deemed to be economic. This is a great mistake. The problem of raising the lower order in India is not to feed them, to clothe them, and make them serve the higher order as is the ancient ideal of this country. The problem of the lower order is to remove from them that inferiority complex which has stunted their growth and made them slaves to others, to create in them the consciousness of the significance of their lives for themselves and for the country, of which they have been robbed by the existing social order. Nothing

can achieve this except the spread of higher education. This in my opinion is the panacea of our social troubles".

Vitality of such quotation still holds true as indifferent attitude of other students towards Scheduled caste students affects their positive self image and participation (Gorettilourdes:2002). In such a scenario, it becomes crucial to look critically towards the present trend of the scheduled caste students' enrollment in higher education.

Impact of Privatization on Scheduled Caste Students

Effect of privatization in higher education is negatively related to the enrollment of all students who are deprived economically, and if we narrow down ourselves to broad participation of the students of scheduled caste community which has been and is encountering discrimination on multiple grounds, then it will act no better than a 'black hole' restraining even a single ray of hope relating to their involvement in higher education. This can be said after looking towards their (SCs') participation in higher education which is dismally low despite having constitutional provision of reservation of 15 per cent as proportional to their population in total population. The present situation is that the scheduled caste is having a share of 16 per cent of the total population of India (Census, 2001) while their enrolment in higher education is merely 7 per cent (SES). If we analyze the entire scenario of higher education in India, the fact remains that only 6 per cent of the relevant age group is in higher education and they do hail from the top 20 per cent of India's socio-economic group is a clear proof education in general and higher education in particular continues to be the preserve of upper castes and classes (Pinto, 2000).

India since time immemorial is a state with multiple diversities and continues to exist with multiple castes or communities having diversified points from low to high on the development scale. Scheduled castes[12] which otherwise are known by several denigrated terms as *'dalits', 'depressed', etc.,* are most disadvantaged (socially) and thus are at the lowest rung on the hierarchical society as exists in India. Apart from social discrimination, the people belonging to this community suffer on the economic vantage point.

Therefore the need for the state to provide the students of this community a safeguard such that it becomes possible for them to possess the skills imparted on behalf of higher education. This will help in transformation of these, which are supposed to be a liability for the state into assets and hence widening the base for the knowledge based society, a prerequisite for better survival in the technically globalised world.

Impact of the market oriented policies, which were implemented informally from the mid 80s and formally from the early 90s, has been grossly negative on them (Teltumbde, 2008). Market enthusiasts only relate the poor through 'Trickle down Theory' according to which the development of benefits of market will get trickled down to the bottom most layer of the society, which has actually not happened. It is important to remember here that on the basis of such premise the world has witnessed most powerful earthquake on the economic scale in the form of 'Great Depression' of 1930s and J.M. Keynes came to rescue with recommendation of state support in various sectors of economy.

Market oriented policies have affected scheduled caste into two ways:

1. They have eroded the constitutional space that signifies the current mode of their existence.
2. They have marred their long term project of emancipation.

There has been a conscious drive towards marketization of higher education through the various initiatives that the government has taken. The thrust of the change could be clearly discerned in terms of confining the governments' role to literacy so that people don't fall out of the market net and get higher education entirely in the private domain for a select few who can afford its commercial costs. Thus increasing costs of education and drying up education due to 'no job' specters led to undoing of positive effects of reservation. Moreover the market reforms have created a neo caste divide in education, which is affectingly pushing dalits back into the dark times that held them as slaves for centuries (Teltumbde, 2008).

Significance of the Problem

In the present century, knowledge based society has become crucial for the real development of the state. Higher education is essentially required to establish such society. And 'inclusiveness' of all the sections of the society holds the key importance to enlarge knowledge base in the existing society of the state. India is a state with diversified society where different sections were hierarchically placed till 1950 when in constitution the concept of 'equality' was conspicuously placed and thereafter several measures were taken to reduce the inequalities in every sector of the state. SCs that were economically deprived and socially discriminated were the major attention seeker of the constitution makers and therefore positive discrimination in form of 'reservation' was provided to them along with other deprived section(s) in all the sectors. During the period of more than fifty years from 1950 various studies have been undertaken to notice the enrollment of SCs in higher education to judge if their participation is sufficient according to their population level. All the studies done in this respect showed that the enrolment and participation of SC community in higher education is far less than satisfactory. Since 1991 the state of India has followed policy of liberalization in the higher education where 'privatization' is allowed to dispense education. It becomes important to assess the enrolment and participation of SC students in higher education after coming of privatization.

With this backdrop the present study is an attempt to analyze the phenomenon of 'privatization' in Indian higher education. Also the study will try to explore the impact of such phenomenon on the enrolment trend of SC students pursuing higher education and whether it has reduced the existing disparity in comparison with General category students. Further the study will see the parity level in the enrolment trends of SC girls' vis-à-vis their male counterparts.

Statement of the Problem

Education is the only entity that marks emphatic demarcation between civilization and barbarism. The higher one gets education the more is the acquisition of the skills to earn a better living. Therefore, higher education becomes indispensable in the present globalised world economy to enhance the returns getting capability from the life. India is a state with bounties of nature and varied diversities along with a common hierarchical society. Scheduled castes remaining at the lowest rung since time immemorial, was deprived of opportunity to be enlightened. And recently after getting independence through various constitutional provisions, these communities under the aegis of the state, were given chance to 'be' what they aspired for through education in general while higher education in particular. Since the last decade of the 20th century as a result of 'globalization', Indian states followed the policy of liberalization which led to the increased share of privatization in the mixed socialist economy.

In this context the present study is undertaken to reveal the fact regarding impact of privatization on the participation of the SC students in the higher education. The purpose of the study is to analyze the phenomenon of 'privatization' in higher education in India. Further the study will assess the SC's enrolment in higher education in different states of India for the last fifteen years in different courses and at various levels.

Definition of Key Terms

Higher Education

Education that is imparted after the senior secondary stage i.e. after completion of 12th standard comes under the category of higher education. Though the term 'higher education' encapsulates varied disciplines and courses, however for this study the higher education will include general education i.e. science, commerce, and arts streams at under and professional education i.e. engineering, medical, and education at various levels.

Scheduled Castes

Comprising of various castes within the broad community of 'scheduled caste' or the 'Dalits' were previously (prior to independence) considered outcastes and were excluded from the chaturvarna system that was the social superstructure of Hindu society in the Indian subcontinent. These castes have traditionally been relegated to the most menial labour with no possibility of upward mobility and are subject to extensive social disadvantage and discrimination by the other categories of 'chaturvarna system' in 1935 the British passed the govt. of India act which brought the term 'scheduled caste' into use and comprised various castes, races or tribes, which were formerly under the category of depressed class. As per the 2001 census the population is over 16 per cent. These had been provided by the constitution safeguard in the form of reservation of 15 per cent in all public institutions and authorities.

Privatization

In the crude terms 'privatization' implies doing away with the control of the 'public' on the state govt. In education there has been categorization of private institutions in India as—aided and unaided, on the basis of aid (in the form) of funds received by the institute by the govt. With the policy of 'Liberalization, Privatization and Globalization' (LPG) after 1991, the govt. paved the way for the privatization i.e. private educational institutions in India. Such institutions have increased over the years (Anandakrishnan, 2006).

Objectives

The basic aim of this study is to investigate the phenomenon of 'privatization' in higher educational sector in India. The study also tries to note down the trends of enrolment of SC students in higher education for different states of India. In this manner, the study examines impact of privatization on the enrolment of SC students and compares it with that of General category students. Further, it also notices the impact of privatization on the parity level among SC students at higher education.

The specific objectives of the study are as follows:

- To analyze the various government policies mentioned in NPE'86, 92 and in various Five Year Plans about the higher education and its impact on SC students.
- To study the enrolment pattern of SCs in both general and professional higher education.
- To study the existing gap between SC and General category students in terms of enrolment in higher education in different courses at various levels in different states of India.
- To study the existing parity level among the SC category in higher education.

Research Questions

- What are the implications of privatization of higher education in India?
- What are the enrolment trends of SCs in higher education since 1991?
- Whether there are gaps in terms of enrolment of SC students when compared with the General category students in different disciplines of higher education?
- What are the growth rates of SC students in higher education at different levels in various disciplines?
- Does the gender parity exist in higher education among SC category?

Delimitations of the Study

- The study has used only secondary data.
- The study was not spread to all the states of India as related data were not available for the same.
- Due to the bifurcation of the states of U.P., Bihar, and M.P. in the year 2000, distinct study for these states was not possible.

Notes

1. Definition of 'Social Exclusion' offered by European foundation (as cited by Naila Kabeer) is:
   "[S]ocial exclusion is the process through which individuals or groups are wholly or partially excluded from full participation in the society in which they live."
2. Concept derived from Ashwani Saith, as mentioned by Naila Kabeer.
3. World Bank Report, 1994: The development of higher education is correlated with economic development: enrollment ratios in higher education average 51 percent in countries that belong to the Organization of Economic Cooperation and Development (OECD), compared with 21 percent in middle income countries and 6 percent in low income countries. Estimated social returns of 10 percent or more in developing countries also indicate that investments in higher education contributed to increase in labour productivity and to higher long term economic growth, which are essential for poverty eradication.
4. Richard A. Musgrave (1959): Theory of Public Finance, McGraw Hill, New York, And Also in (1987): "merit goods,", "The New Palgrave: A Dictionary of Economics", v. 3, pp. 452-53.
5. Idem as cited by Head, 1969.
6. As cited by Ravinder Singh (2005) Privatization of Higher Education in the Era of Globalization, *University News* 43(34) pp. 9-13.
7. Justice R.C.Lahoti, Preamble: The spirit and backbone of the constitution of India 2 (Lucknow: Eastern Book Co., 2004).
8. Article 38(2) states that the state shall strive to promote public welfare by securing a social order in which social, economic, and political justice informs all institutions of national life. Article 38(2) spells out minimization of inequality in status, facilities and opportunities, as a goal to be attained through state action. Similarly, Article 39 desires the operation of the economic system without concentration of wealth and means of production. It also envisages the distribution of ownership and control of material resources in a manner best serving the common good.
9. Article 41: The state shall, within the limits of economic capacity and development, make effective provision for securing the right to work, to education, and to public assistance in cases of unemployment, old age, sickness, and disablement, and in other cases of undeserved want.

10. Article 46: The state shall promote with special care the educational and economic interests of the weaker sections of the people, and in particular of the scheduled castes and the scheduled tribes, and shall protect them from social injustice and all forms of exploitation.
11. Psacharopoulos and Patrinos (2004) argue that for developing countries, priority should be given to achieve universal primary education, while concomitantly; innovative means of financing lifelong earnings for those who are employed should top the policy agenda. However, the use of rate of return approach for guiding investment decisions in education has been subject to criticism (Majumdar, 1983). Investment in education is sequential in character as students pass from one stage to another stage. Furthermore, investment in education need not be compared with investments in other sectors like transport and power because benefits of education cut across sectoral boundaries and it is important for intrinsic values.
12. The Government of India Act 1935 brought the term "Scheduled Castes" into vogue and use and defined the group as including "such castes, races or tribes or parts of groups within castes, races or tribes, which appear to His Majesty in council to correspond to the classes of persons formerly known as the 'Depressed Classes', as His Majesty Council may prefer". This discretionary definition was clarified in the Government of India (Scheduled Castes), 1936 which contained a list or schedule, of castes throughout the British administered provinces.

    After Independence, the Constituent Assembly continued the prevailing definition of Scheduled Castes and Tribes, and gave (via articles 341, 342) the President of India and Governors of states responsibility to compile a full listing of castes and tribes and also the power to edit it later as required.

2

Relevance of the Issue

Reflection through Literature and Methodolgy

The existing literature available on the various issues is organized in a manner that entire review of the related researches and arguments, is categorized into three sections. The first section will look into the importance of higher education while the second and third section will respectively deal with privatization of higher education in India and its implications for the scheduled caste students where the latter will also take into consideration the studies conducted for the enrolment pattern of scheduled caste students in higher education in India. Also, a brief review has been attempted at the last to have a glance over the participation of scheduled caste students in higher education. This may enhance the support for the reforms needed to make their endeavor to complete higher education a success.

Importance of Higher Education

Various researches are there to establish the importance of higher education for the development of the state and for social cohesion. In this respect Castells (1991) states the purpose of higher education, which is provided in the universities as means of personal growth for the individual, means of constructing culture, sharing traditions and providing well being for the society as a whole and as a means of accumulating personal and social wealth and competitiveness (see e.g. Bowen 1980, 55-59, Scott 1998, 111).

Further, Sadlak (1998) cites world bank statistics of 1994 in pointing out that there is a distinct correlation between rates of participation in higher education and the overall economic development of countries: the rate of participation in higher education in OECD, representing 30 of the wealthiest countries in the world, in the beginning of 1990s was 51 per cent compared with 21 per cent of middle income countries and 61 per cent of developing countries. Elaborating the function of higher education to establish equality, Verghese (2001) analyzed the persistent inequalities in the world through regression analysis and points out that looking various statistics of enrolment level and development (in real terms) it is clear that the more the enrolment in higher education the more developed an economy is. Based on his study of trends around the world, Verghese stated that once higher education reaches Massification or universal stage, its impact on equality becomes positive and significant. Therefore, the need in developing countries like India is to universalize higher education by making it more inclusive and democratic.

Privatization of Higher Education in India

Regarding the issue of privatization of higher education there are ample number of literature available that tries to explore privatization of higher education from both negative as well as positive aspect. Also, there are studies that try to look at the whole issue in the Indian context, answering the questions about efficiency, efficacy, and feasibility in order to establish socialist society as mentioned in the constitution of India.

From various studies Dixon (2006) points out that there are three types of privatization i.e. (a) Demand side financing in which reforms like introduction of targeted vouchers are made, (b) Supply side where reforms include Public funding of a new or existing private schools (e.g. in Europe, Frasse *et al.*; 1987; Dronkers, 1995; Ritzen *et al.*; 1997; Karsten, 1999), (c) De facto Privatization i.e. transfer of authority to private sector. After having categorized privatization into three broad categories in terms of education, Tooley & Dixon (2006) have supported the private education at the school level on the basis of research conducted in Sub- Saharan countries and India. Though they have presented the facts that equity issue could be easily managed under private authority but the authors remain unaware about the drawbacks as mismanagement and social biases that exist in India. The authors in their study didn't mention about community from where students are coming to the school in Hyderabad and Mahbubnagar; and also didn't mention their presence at different parameters utilized in study as teaching activity, pupil achievement, etc.

Taking 'privatization' to higher education in India, Chauhan (2004) has shown that there are various benefits of privatization as otherwise the poor people are paying for the education of elite (in form of subsidies which comes through indirect taxes) as only the latter are opting for higher education as per the trend. However the author failed to take note of the ill effects of privatization of the higher education in India as it will maintain the social status quo keeping the unprivileged out of the ambit of higher education. This is further discussed by Tilak (1997) who mentions that in all the public policies on education major question which comes across is who should pay for education, which has been further strengthened by the policy of economic reforms. After the liberalization, privatization, Globalization policies, consideration for equity has been sacrificed for efficiency. The poor does not figure in any discussion for financing of education as if education is a luxury good meant only for the rich. The author mentions that scholarship and student loan programmes have not served as antidote to the regressive effects of increases in fees as they are associated with inherent administrative and structural weaknesses.

Government policy of public expenditure since independence has led to massive expansion of the system at all levels. The higher education was transformed from an elitist system of the 1950s to the mass based higher education by the 1990s. However after giving sanctions to privatization it seems the previous trend will be established after some time undoing the benefits previously done. Also, the author thinks that privatization of higher education can't be an acceptable policy as it will lead to commercialization where whoever will invest would do so with a profit motive and not with a motive of social development or advancement in education.

Tracing the higher education in India right from ancient period and presenting its present structure, Jayaram (2004) focused on the challenges faced by the same in the wake of liberalization of government policies. The author clearly accepts that privatization in higher education has resulted from the government's policy in consonance with structural adjustment reforms. This has turned higher education dearly keeping the mass of people away from its ambit. The increasing cost of higher education makes it less accessible to the masses and also adversely affects the quality of education if the government doesn't regulate the private educational institutions. The author states that privatization is sure to reinforce existing inequalities and to foster in egalitarian tendencies.

Agarwal (2007) makes a clear distinction in the face of higher education in India with 1980 as a watershed year, after which there has been growth of private institutions in India albeit the growth accelerated after 1990s. This has been the result of various factors as increase in demand, lack of funds, decline in philanthropy, etc. However, there is a weak regulatory structure in the private funding as Supreme Court has to intervene for the future of 50000 students. The author points out that the major flaw in financial scenario in public universities is uneven support from government as major chunk goes to reputed institutions while other institutes are striving for funds making higher education dearly and thus fail to tale into consideration equity aspect. The entire scenario is helping in mushrooming of private institutions and Gresham's law is kicking in and bad is driving out the good. Therefore Pawan Agarwal suggests for more investment from public funds on higher education.

Giving the political angle to privatization of higher education in India, Mehta & Kapur (2004) have examined the political economy of higher education in India and said the present day privatization is not any requirement or is not a result of change in ideology for good, rather it is because of breakdown of the state system and an exit of Indian elites from public institutions to both private sectors in country and abroad. They have pointed towards inapt governance that has reduced the quality and autonomy of institutes leading to decline in philanthropy and towards direct privatization.

Patel (2004) gives importance to the higher education in India and states that there is political inefficiency which is making the way for privatization. Kumar (2004) as cited in (Patel, 2004), mentions that if the Black Economy (40 per cent of the GDP) is tapped and taxed the state would have enough liquid funds to invest in education. The author favours for public control over higher education as private fund will serve private interests as seen in Birla Ambani Reports' recommendations. The author said privatization which is, an offshoot of globalization phenomenon, will do great harm to higher education as it is leading towards commoditization of the same in spite of imparting knowledge.

Gupta (2005) in her occasional paper titled 'International Trends in Private Higher Education and the Indian Scenario' mentions that higher education in India has to be left to the private players under the competitive pressures on the economy in the wake of Structural Adjustment Programs. This is to be done as there is increasing debt over Indian government. This logic is refuted by Narayana (2006) who has analyzed privatization by doing study in the state of Karnataka. He finds that 'Pure Privatization' i.e. complete control by private authorities of higher education will have marginal effect on fiscal i.e. only 6.12 per cent of fiscal deficit will be covered, while it will increase the student fees in general higher education by 21 times leading to drop out by poor background students. This policy will affect adversely to the backward communities like SCs, and therefore suggests for post privatization controls as accreditation, regulations, etc. by the government authorities. Such instruments as 'Golden Share' by government have been successful in OECD countries to promote national interests.

Issue of establishing equality in the state also becomes important as has been analyzed by different authors. Kaul (1993) opines that privatization of higher education will perpetuate inequalities in the system. Economic inequalities will accentuate inequalities in access to higher education which in turn contributes to the inequalities to occupational achievements, in earnings and in socio-economic sphere as whole. Higher education, the 'public' or the 'Quasi-Public good' will turn out to be a 'luxury good', and the middle and even upper middle income classes may not afford it. It will become monopoly of the rich. Regarding 'quality', Kaul reports that only 1/3 of the students feel that facilities provided and also the faculty in these institutions were of 'poor quality'. Also, FICCI Survey (2006) on Understanding of Private Higher Education in India reveals that students of private Higher Educational Institutes are less satisfied with the course curricula than those in government institutes. Also, in the study, majority of the respondents wanted government accreditation of private institutes. The major limitation of the study is that it fails to address the social problem of inequality in access to higher education in India.

It has been further found by different scholars that privatization at higher level of education contributes to persistence of socio-economic inequalities in the society, providing the elitist bias in education Walford & Kaul (1990). Also, the complete Marketization of higher education would go against the constitutional obligation of providing equal opportunities of education to all at different levels. It also acts as a *'social lift agent'* (Mehta, 1993).

Comparing the systems of higher education worldwide, Altbach (1999) establishes the fact that privatization does exists in different nations albeit in various proportions e.g. in Republic of Korea, Japan and East European nations it has a major composition while in western Europe, etc. has proportionately lower contribution for the private sector. Also, the nature of privatization varies across the nations. While some are having privatization with public funds, others have autonomous sort of privatization depending upon legal framework a state is equipped with.The author points out that at present the trend among all the nations is to privatize the higher education in a manner that it yields profit which is private to the large extent. In this scenario, various challenges are needed to be addressed as question of equity, inclusiveness with which there are related issues as quality, autonomy, etc. Though the author has presented view of low economic background of a student(s) which a pro-profit privatization fails to address, it fails to mention the peculiar dimension of social discrimination which can't be undone by the elitist private higher educational institutions.

Referring to the article13 of the International Covenant on Economic, Social, and Cultural Rights in 1973 which emphasizes over efforts by the states to make higher education accessible to all, Mark Bray (2000) mentions that by 1990 this clause was abandoned in the view that only elite are going for higher education which is funded through taxes paid by the non-elitist group of people. Therefore the trend to reduce public expenditure on higher education began. Taking view of Indian universities, Mark Bray points out that major portion of the recurrent income came from government grants. This will shift to student fees in case of privatization.

Analyzing privatization in various countries, Tilak (2005) mentions that the privatization has brought drastic adverse change in the higher education system in the developing nations particularly vis-à-vis the developed nation as the participation rate of youths in the former is already dismal. Also, he mentions that with the coming of privatization the role of higher education has shifted to profit-making from the generator of knowledge, an instrument to empowerment and social engineering. In the article, the author mentions that the doctrine of laissez-faireism, which means minimum state intervention and allowing of activities to take their own natural course, was described by Thomas Carlyle as "anarchy plus the constable". Since the constable is weak, we have only anarchy in the higher education scene in developing countries.

Some scholars have taken the aspect of returns attached to the higher education. In this regard, Psarcharopoulos (1994) showed that private returns of education are more than social returns at all levels as governments give more subsidies than they take away in in taxes. Refuting such argument, Tilak (1997a) on the basis of evidence showed that private rates of returns are falling over time. Also, criticizing Psacharopoulos, Mingat and Tan (1996), said that it's difficult to estimate externalities. They aimed to estimate the "full" social returns to education in Economies with different strengths. By the "full" social returns, Mingat and Tan meant calculations that allow for the many externalities that accrue to whole societies and that are not normally taken into account by studies that merely aggregate the returns to individuals.

The higher education in India shows a dismal picture with a low enrolment ratio in respect to the respective population. Oza (1999) states that though the enrolment is large (in figures) in India thanks to its population size, actually it hardly covers 6 percent of young people in the age group of 18-23 years. This is dismally low in comparison with 51 percent in the OECD countries. Among the non-enrolled are the disadvantaged youth from weaker sections and from rural and remote areas. Also, though the number of students in professional institutions like IIMS, IITs, IIITs, Agricultural Universities, etc. has increased, however the majority is still going to general first degree programmes in humanities and social sciences. This has necessitated the need for government intervention in higher education which is vitally important for the economic, social, and cultural development in the wake of globalization (Periyasamy, 2004).

Regarding financing of higher education, the government spends 15 percent of the educational allotment or 0.6 percent of GNP. A discussion paper (GOI, 1997) entitled "Government subsidies in India", identifies the spending on higher education as non-merit subsidy. The author states that it is clear from the going trends that privatization of higher education essentially means increasing reliance on private sources of educational finance in place of ever increasing government subsidies. However, the importance which the higher education is holding doesn't permit the government to withdraw completely from financing the higher education. The author has suggested measures as inclusion of alumni, industry, philanthropists, trusts, and endowments Oza (1999).

Recent trend of financing higher education India, Mukherjee (2008) gives figure of declining public share in higher education. In terms of GDP, from 1990-91 to 2004-05, the share of higher education fell from 0.77 per cent to 0.66 per cent in real terms, per student expenditure made by the government declined 28 per cent from 1990-91 to 2002-03. On the basis of NASSCOM-McKinsey study of 2005, the author fears of adverse implications on quality of higher education under private auspices, as the main intention then is to earn more profit through capitation fees.

Establishing facts about financing of higher education, Sharma (1989) states that in a mixed economy like India, education is a 'social-merit good' which is different from 'merit' and 'social' good, concept utilized in capitalist and socialist framework respectively. In the concept of 'merit' good, the state intervenes to correct the failures of market forces while in 'social' good concept, state intervention is total. In a mixed economy, there is a socialistic pattern of society where education is considered a key input for economic and social development with justice, and therefore adequate financial provisions from economy should be made for education. Also, there should be adequate provisions for students from the weaker sections of the society.

Impact of Privatization of Higher Education on Scheduled Castes

After studying the available literature on privatization of higher education in India it is required to see the literature showing impact of privatization in higher education on Scheduled Caste students in order to achieve the objective of the study. With the coming of unfettered privatization (Chalam, 2004) in higher education in India, the major issue of concern is collapsing of reservation policies to the Scheduled Caste students which are hitherto available. Therefore the related literature taken for the present study will have prime focus over reservation policies of SC students in higher education.

Weisskopf (2004) in '*Impact of Reservation on Admissions to Higher Education in India*', presents extensive view on the reservation for Scheduled Caste and Scheduled Tribe candidates particularly after 1990s when after LPG *(Liberalization, Privatization, Globalization)* policies were announced by the government, there has been mushrooming of different private institutions which do not take care of the interests of these deprived sections. Through figures he present that though the reservation policy marking positive discrimination for SCs and STs and other deprived candidates was announced in 1950s, none of the universities had paid heed to it and was thus not implemented before 1970s and 1980s in various government institutes. Also, Weisskopf gives view that reservation to be effectively given at primary and secondary level and the reservation at the higher education is basically an effort to promote integration of upper strata of society by increasing to access to the disadvantaged to the elite possessions.

Presenting the logic of reservation in higher education which is only available in the public institutes, Weisskopf (2004) states, without reserved seats, the appeal of a higher educational institution for SC and ST potential students is likely to be substantially diminished. Also, such admission enhances the ability of such student(s) to gain access to financial and other forms of government aid(s) needed for their development. However, the author, utilizing various reports and draft papers as by Velaskar (Inequality in higher education—a study of SC students in medical colleges of Bombay, a Ph.D Dissertation:1986), Rao (Equality in higher education: Impact of Affirmative action policies in India, unpublished draft paper, JNU:2001), and Sinha (The Harijan Elite, Thomson press, New Delhi:1977), has mentioned that the reservation at the same time is creating a hierarchy among different reserved categories as the benefit is utilized by the few elites among such categories. This has been refuted by Mendelson & Vicziamy, 1998), who take the issue of 'social discrimination' as more important which is being faced by the entire reserved community of scheduled castes.

Teltumbde (2007) in 'State, Market and Dalits' presents a view that with globalization market has become the sole decider of every activity that is happening in the state and marketization of higher education is a part of it. With this there has been increasing cost of education and drying up of motivation for education due to no job sector leading to undoing of the positive effects of reservation. It is stated that the supporters of market believe that benefits of market will get trickled down to the bottom most layer of the society which has actually not happened. It is important to remember that on the basis of such premise the world has witnessed the most powerful earthquake on economic scale in the form of 'Great Depression'

Reservation argument has been also supported by Thorat (2005) who in his article '*Why Reservation is Necessary?*' says that with the announcement of LPG policies in the era of Globalization it becomes conspicuous that reservation is important to ensure participation of Scheduled Caste students in higher education. Therefore the author has recommended for providing reservation in the privately established institutes by the government to undo the doubly disadvantage of this community.

Importance has been attached to various protective government policies such as reservation by Chitnis (1976) in her study on Scheduled Caste students in colleges in Bombay where she found that among the major problems these students were facing was of financial deprivation and academic deficiency. In such circumstances, reservation policies are inevitable solution which would collapse under private ambit.

Taking a different route to analyze educational participation of SCs in higher education, Akhoury (2008) in her article '*Impact of Globalization on Dalits*' has explicitly placed different dimension of the problem of Dalits where interconnectedness of different social, economic, and educational aspect has been showed. It is mentioned that how dalits devoid of land in the era globalization are more disadvantaged. In the globalized era, there is more commercialization of various skills which one can ascertain through professional education. And such education proved for these disadvantaged groups as forbidden fruit despite the availability of various scholarships at the traditional universities. The result is that the majority of the graduating candidates of the deprived community (ies) add to the figures of unorganized labour where there is a lack of social safety net. Akhoury has also stated that with the coming of Globalization, opportunity cost to have education for the Dalits has gone up as they could have gainful employment in lieu of getting education required to have specialized skills which is much dearer now under privatization.

Tilak (1991) has exposed the hollowness of various myths about 'Privatization as a better means' by juxtaposing it with the empirical evidences around the world. With facts from various countries as Japan, Philippines, Thailand, etc. where privatization is existing in big way, Tilak proves that privatization which is moved by the sole profit motive, in isolation is neither efficient nor can serve as a true agent for distributive justice. The author propounds a model which is mixed in nature of ownership by public and private authorities, to take into consideration both the social and private returns from higher education which according to him is quasi-public good. However, the author in the article does not emphatically mentions about social disparities that exist in India and how these can be accommodates in the model suggested.

Thinking privatization as inevitable, Sharma (2007) has discussed the NKC report given to Prime Minister in which NKC is concerned about declining public funding for higher education and suggest enhancement in the same. Also, it recommends that public University should use their land to generate funds as a source of finance. For the equity, NKC recommends for 'Deprivation Index' to be formulated and reservation policy should move out. Actually, there are certain limitations of preparing such index which is aptly applicable in case of entrance test only. Moreover, comprehensive index including different caste is a loadsome and flawful exercise in the disparity scenario in India.

Ghosh (2006) favours caste based reservation as an appropriate form of affirmative action in Indian scenario. She mentions that 'deprivation point' seems to be an attractive idea but its workable only under the condition of institutions admitting students on the basis of entrance test, otherwise it seems impossible to carve out a particular scheme for its administration. However she points out that reservation in the higher educational institute as a panacea for undoing the injustices that had done to the deprived sections in the society which ultimately had led to an in egalitarian or rater hierarchical society. Admitting deprived students to higher education is the most workable method as suggested by Ghosh (2006).

It is further pointed out by Ghosh (2006) that inclusiveness and not exclusion makes a market and economy competitive and much more efficient contrary to the discriminatory policy followed in India e.g. countries like Malaysia, which combine a very severe and restrictive form of reservation and other affirmative action with remarkable economic growth for several decades.

Teltumbde (2008) in the article has mentioned that with the coming of globalization there has begun an era of commercialization of education which adversely affects the dalit students. Therefore the requirement is to have assistance from government in various forms, otherwise even today; it would be difficult even for the 2nd generation educated dalits to send their children to school.

Emphasizing reservation policy in Indian higher education, Deshpande (2008) says that reservation or quota is required for social justice. The author clearly demarcates between social prejudice and economic deprivation, in order to support the cause for social injustice. Also, the issue of merit is very much subjective as told by the author. The 'merit' argument, author states is basically utilized to nullify the competence of one group of students. Also, the concept of merit in concept and force depends on its vision of good society which is based on the perception about the same.

Based on his various findings related to enrolment and attainment of higher education across different socio-religious communities which reflect a deficit in the category of SCs, Basant (2008) suggests that reservation in higher education is an incentive to cross the threshold. Similarly, job reservation can enhance the incentives to participate in higher education.

Deshpande and Yadav (2006) support the point of providing reservations to the backward communities as they are lagging behind in the race of development if the indicator of access and participation of these in education as a whole is considered. However the authors wanted to alter the policy of implementation of reservation policies based on caste quotas with policy on providing deprivation points while admitting them in the institutions. This will provide comprehensive benefits to the disadvantaged communities deprived on various points as gender, locality, etc.

Mehta & Hasan (2006) bring the issue of 'democracy' as validity for the affirmative action for equal participation or rather for equality of opportunity to all. Further he states that issue of 'merit' is subjective and thinks the processing part in the institution as more important for defining or redefining merit. The author holds opinion of basing a policy to build every institution of quality standard which could consider the aspect of diversity and can provide access to all. All this exercise can make the reservation policy truly successful.

Pointing towards reform needed in the government policy towards 'Dalits', Choudhary (1998) states that in NPE'86 and POA'92, the issue of SCs has been neglected and does not find any mention in the entire document in clear terms. Also, in the 9th FYP, the government favoured for privatization which would keep educational equality/equity at the stake.

Further the author has criticized the model given by Dr. Ambrose Pinto in the paper 'Dalits in Higher Education: Need for Establishing Counter Culture', where a separate institution for SCs is recommended. This would lead to drastic consequence against the development of dalits and would make way for fragmentation.

Commenting on government's educational policy, Chalam (2008) has said that the NPE'86 and POA'92 though clearly talks about elementary education of dalits but such policies are silent on higher and professional education of the same. Hinting towards ill-effects of privatization of higher education the author mentions that previously the report formulated by Birla and Ambani has never mentioned the interests of the dalits as the motive under such set up remains profit and has excluded the underprivileged dalits. The author mentions clearly that for real development higher education should be provided to all and those can't afford it should not remain excluded.

The author has rightly mentioned that education in India is neither an economic problem nor purely an educational issue. It is a social enigma. Social exclusion is structurally constructed which can't be undone unless these are dismantled.

Social exclusion is a unique innovation that has an Indian patent and can be tinkered with the policy of positive discrimination. Chalam (2008) stressed on the importance of higher education and therefore state's control over it such that no one remains disadvantaged. He cites example of Britain which has reversed its policy of liberalization in higher education. There the secretary of state Charles Clarke has declared to raise budget for higher education from 7.5 billion pounds in 2003 to 10 billion pounds in 2005-06.

Enrolment and Participation of Scheduled Caste Students in Higher Education in India

From the available educational statistics, it is well established that the enrolment and participation of Scheduled Caste students in higher education in general and technical education in particular, is far from satisfactory. This is so when different constitutional clauses explicitly emphasizes over the participation of the educationally backward communities like scheduled castes. And hence there is positive discrimination in their favour.

Prakash (2008) through his study of various statistics made it clear that drop out rate among SCs and STs at class 8 and 10 is quite high. It is 55 and 63 per cent at class 8, and 71 and 79 per cent at class 10 for SCs and STs respectively in 2005-06. This makes the picture of their enrolment at higher educational level quite disappointing. He points out that the enrolment per cent of SCs in higher education is 12.3 in 2005-06 which has increased from 8.5 in 1990-91. And this growth is due to interventions by government in the form of reservation policy and various incentives as scholarships, freeships, hostel facility, etc. However, their proportion is much below in professional courses as engineering, medical, etc. With the coming of privatization, such development would be hampered and social engineering process would be stalled if not stopped. Therefore the author suggests the manifold increase in public funding and to contain the process of commercialization of education.

Bhatt (2005) mentions that as per the information from Selected Education Statistics of various years on enrolment of Scheduled Castes from 1995 to 1998, its clear that there has been a decline in courses of Arts, Science and Medicine at the undergraduate level. The total enrolment figures (excluding professional and technical courses) declined from 8.91 in 1995-96 to 8.72 in 1998-99. The states which showed negative growth are Manipur, Delhi, Karnataka, West Bengal, Gujarat, Daman & Diu, Kerala, Arunachal Pradesh, and Maharashtra, Assam, Bihar and U.P. On the basis of his research findings the author mentions that though the literacy level, which has crucial effect on the enrolment in higher education, has increased among the scheduled castes' students since independence but the disparity with non-Scheduled caste students has increased in these years. Also, the author point out that coefficient of equality of scheduled caste with non-scheduled castes has declined at the increased level of education. In 1995 itself it was 102.10 at primary level which has increased to 54.49 at higher education level. It implies that wastage and stagnation among SCs are quite high.

From his own findings he shows that SC students are underrepresented in higher educational institutes and are below their population proportion i.e. 15 per cent. Though the author fails to find any appropriate reason for such a low representation, it recommends for a critical review by the UGC for their participation which may help the government in formulating policy to the cause. It can be emphasized that if such is the scenario under government aegis the situation under private authorities won't be improving as the motive would be solely private profit.

From various studies done earlier on different aspects of SC students affecting their well-being and also on social integration, Chatterjee (2000) proves that educational development of SCs is certainly having positive results. The trend report of NCERT in 1978-83 reveals that the participation of the enrolled students at the school level is low, also studies as done by Abbasayulu (1978) in Hyderabad point towards their education as a means to enhance their status. Also, there seems to have a positive correlation of education of SCs with the reduced family size (Jain&Moni, 1987). Also, various studies as done by Chitnis (1981), Malik (1979), Prajapati (1982), etc. has shown that increase in the educational achievement at lower level leads to higher aspirations among the SC students. Thus it is a way for having better enrolments of SCs in higher education.

Chalam (1988) after studying the enrolment of SC students as given in various secondary sources found that there is an increase in enrolment. But this is due to participation by groups who can afford it. Also it was found that the per cent of SC students is more at elementary stage which decreases at higher level. In the same study it was found that there is a high enrolment of SC students in higher education in the state of Andhra Pradesh. This according to him can be attributed to more number of Christians in the SC category in developed districts which grabs the opportunity of reservation to the SC category.

Aggarwal and Sibou (1994) had conducted study on the basis of secondary enrolment data for period between 1964 and 1977 for SC students in higher education. From the study it comes out that there is an increase in enrolment in higher education, but such enrolment increase is mostly concentrated in arts course.

Gorettilourdes (2002) with her study on SC students in MS University found out that student in different disciplines at the undergraduate and post-Graduate level, had above average achievement. However, she points out that one of the finding in her study was that the students suffer from anxiety due to indifferent attitude of other students towards them making the feel low which also could have hampered their achievement. The author clarifies that their academic achievement has its relation with the assistance and surveillance of government in the form of reservation, freeships, hostel facilities, etc. The study makes it clear that government ownership of institutes of higher learning is required for benefitting the hitherto deprived community of SC students and the privatization could hamper their real growth.

Patwardhan & Palshikar (1992) had carried out a large stratified random sample among doctors who graduated from a well known medical college in Pune between 1971 and 1982 and studied career paths of doctors after their graduation. The interesting finding is that reserved seat candidate has seen significant upward mobility on socio-economic scale and that practically all reserved seat candidates were clearly very competent as doctors.

Sinha & Sinha (1989) had done a nationwide survey on the problems of education among SCs and STs. The sample of the study was students studying in colleges and schools located in Bihar and came out with several conclusions. Firstly, the economic backwardness is the major cause of dropping out of the students. Secondly various scholarships available at schools and colleges to the scheduled caste students are the source of financial help in continuing education. Further it was found that social stigma is there and affects in building of relationship among the students of different castes particularly between the scheduled caste students and non-scheduled caste students.

Aikara (1980) has done study on the college students in Bombay to find out cause for their stagnation and drop outs. On the basis of his study, he concluded that SC students in the college are weak academically which is the result of their financial backwardness. He suggests that financial assistance and the reservation of seats are two factors that can lead to the enrollment of undeserving candidates in the college.

Chitins (1976) as cited in (Malhotra & Rizvi (ed.), 1997) have done a study where a stratified random sample of 122 Non-SC and 185 SC students in 2nd year in Bombay University was taken to know about their problems. It was found that SC students had low financial background and other academic deficiency which is made up through various government policies. Also, higher education of parents is positively related to aspiration for better performance in higher education among SC students.

Mahadeva (2003) through his study of various statistics related to the development of SCs provided by NSSO, CSO, Census, Planning Commission, etc., has presented the impoverished condition of SCs which is reflected in their being landless, appointed at lower grade jobs, deprived of basic amenities, etc. This has a bearing on their dismal participation at all levels of education. He recommends for affirmative action by the public authorities.

The study conducted by Premi (1983) as cited in (Malhotra & Rizvi, 1997) shows disparities between SCs and non SCs in different states indicating the emerging trend, however the period of study is restricted between 1964 and 1977.

On the basis of NSSO figures, Ghosh (2008) points out that SC student in rural areas lag behind even STs. She suggests for public action and reservation along with other incentives and facilities like public provision of higher education in backward areas, etc. for making the affirmative action a success. The data reveals of discrimination and marginalization in higher education especially in rural areas.

The author states that private or foreign education is not a panacea for Indian Education system, yet it could bring hope by working locally. Without putting an emphasis over the problems as access and equity, the author points that regulations needed to be revised by government authorities favouring foreign participation.

Participation of SC Students in Higher Education

Several measures have been undertaken enabling participation of the Scheduled Caste students in the higher education. There are facilities and incentives as post matric scholarships, reservation at all levels of higher education and in the hostels, remedial training, and special cells in the institutions of higher learning. However, their situation continues to be grim and away from nearing parity in the wake of simultaneous parallel development of other sections of the society. This is particularly true for the technical and professional education as are majorly concentrated (if at all) in arts and humanities. Such a scenario compels the researchers to delve deeper into the problem in getting various factor(s) that may aid the exclusion despite of having inclusive policies at normative framework.

Various researches have made it clear that there are numerous factors which act as enablers or pose a challenge in participation of students in higher education in general and in technical education at particular level. These factors have serious implications for the participation of scheduled caste students despite the fact their situation is culturally more precarious.

The primary cause of low enrolment and hence participation of Scheduled Caste students is conspicuous from the educational figures which reveal their high drop out at an educational stage which make their eligibility insufficient for getting into higher education, both at general and technical education, very limited. The trend report of NCERT in 1978-83 reveals that the participation of the enrolled students at the school level is low. Further, it has been pointed out from research that pre-enrolment (in university) education with a variable as High School Grade Point plays a crucial role in determining retention of students (Reason, 2009). Also, various studies as done by Chitnis (1981), Malik (1979), Prajapati (1982), Rana & Mehta (2006), has shown that the increase in the educational achievement at lower level leads to higher aspirations among the Scheduled Caste students.

Then, the next most important factor affecting participation of any student in general and Scheduled Caste students particularly, is the socio-economic status of the parents. It is found from the NSS data that economic status counts for the major cause of neglect of higher education among the deprived communities (Rana & Mehta, 2006). It has been noted that low economic status act as a major deprivation in accessing higher education by already deprived students (Sharma, 1974; Rao, 2002; Aggarwal, 2009; Chakrabarty, 2009). And 'economic' crisis demotivate Scheduled Caste students leading to low course complete rate among them (Premi, 1989).

The fact of impact of economic factor on higher education, has also been placed by study conducted in America by Astin & Leticia (2004), where it is found that students of the wealthiest family are overrepresented by factor more than 2 while those from poorest families are underrepresented by a factor of one half, and students of middle income families are underrepresented by a factor of one third. This has been further reiterated by the study conducted (in Australia) by James (2002) where it is revealed that around 70 per cent students from higher socio economic background has shown interest and likelihood to pursue higher education, while it is 50 per cent for middle and 42 per cent for lower socio economic background student. Also, financial aid is the major bottleneck in having confidence and choice for higher education. And in America it was found that high socio economic status (SES) students have almost a 2.5 times chance to pursue education after high school (Sewell, 1971).

In this, it is well stated fact to mention again, that scheduled Caste students have low financial background (Aikara, 1980; Chitnis, 1976). Therefore, it becomes the major cause of dropping out of these students from the education system at all levels (Sachidananda & Sinha, 1989). Also, otherwise, economic inequality has been seen as a major cause of no or neglected participation of students from low or humble economic background. This is due to the fact that economic inequality gets channelized into social and cultural sphere with education as a major component to maintain the existing status quo (Lynch, 2001). This is in continuum of the previous findings by Bourdieu where education is seen as to maintain the existing class differences in the society.

Further, economic disadvantage has certain other manifestations as well like poor management of adolescent's lives by their parents making the less possibility of student's enrolment in higher education later in their life (Crosnoe, Mistry & Glen, 2002). Therefore, economic inequality leads to inequality in enrolment in higher education which gets more emphasized in the case of technical education especially in engineering course. This is in the wake of privatization trend whereby the government share in providing access is declining (Azam & Blom, 2008).

Apart from the economic situation, one of the most significant and peculiar issue to the Scheduled Caste students is ill attitude or antipathy towards them. This has come out as an important issue related to decline in the participation and graduation of SC students particularly at the college level. In the study of three rounds of NSS data, Desai & Kulkarni (2008), found that the decline in graduation of SC students could be additionally attributed to antipathy by fellow students and professors. This confirms the hatred towards dalit students previously found by the study of Sharma (1974) and later by Sachidananda & Sinha (1989). Also, Gorettilourdes (2002) in her study of SC students in M.S.University (Baroda), points that one of the finding was that the students suffer from anxiety due to indifferent attitude of other students towards them. This make them feel low hindering their achievement.

It could be said that such attitude has psychological bearings on the Scheduled Caste students. And it is found that social psychological variable is one of the most significant factors that mediate between academic ability and educational attainment (Sewell, 1971). It helps in 'Goal Commitment' of a student, an essential factor in retention of students in higher education as without this there won't be integration of 'Goal Commitment' and

'Institutional Commitment', leading to drop out (Tinto, 1975). With psychologically inferior feeling, a SC student gets parted from General students in the institute which affects their participation (Kirpal & Gupta, 1985). Such finding also comes out from the empirical studies done by Premi (1989), Sharma (1974), and Schidananda & Sinha (1989), and that of Singh (1989) at school level.

Deficit of 'cultural capital' is another factor which makes Scheduled Caste student disadvantageous vis-à-vis other General category students. Inferior socio-cultural background contributes to lower academic performance (Kirpal & Gupta, 1999). Less of 'cultural capital' due to low educated parents makes less conducive environment for learning (Velaskar, 1986). 'Cultural capital' is important as it is found that the 'sanskritized' lower castes have fared comparatively better in examinations (Parmaji, 1985). One of the major components of 'cultural capital' (that has emerged from various studies) is English language (Velaskar, 1986; Kirpal & Gupta, 1999). Majority of English medium educated comes to IITs irrespective of their community i.e. SCs or Non SCs. However their per centage is much greater in Non SCs (Kirpal & Gupta, 1999).

In relation to culture, parent's motivation is other familial factor that marks its bearing on performance and participation of a student. From the study conducted on successful adolescent development in high risk settings by Crusnoe, Mistry & Glen (2002), it has been found that there is important role played by parent's motivation in form of their perceived efficacy, on parent's positive assessment and thus in enrolment of their child in higher education. Further, it is found that parent's encouragement is a more prominent factor than teacher's encouragement, in influencing student's performance (Sewell, 1971). Alike others, in case of scheduled Caste students, parent's motivation has emerged as major enabling factor to continue higher education (Sachidananda & Sinha, 1989). However, peer group has more significant influence on the performance of student (Sewell, 1971). This could be seen in case of SC students which have low co-curricular participation most probably due to less mingling with General Category students (Sachidananda & Sinha, 1989).

There are several other familial factors which affect the particular participation of Scheduled Caste students either singularly or in cumulative terms. The primary importance could be attached to the family size as there seems positive correlation of education of SC students with the reduced family size (Jain & Moni, 1987). The study on determinants of participation in higher education in India reveals the fact that particularly in case of SC and ST category, an additional child (less than 5 years of age) in the household, proves to be more detrimental for probability of attaining higher education (Chakrabarti, 2009). This acts as a cumulative burden in the case of female child in the same household, particularly in rural areas albeit it is having negative relation for male youth as well (Chakrabarti, 2009). This results in inequality of education on gender lines as all the factor(s) proves to be favourable for male child promoting its education (Sewell, 1971). And it is conspicuously seen in the case of higher education (James, 2002). Such cumulative disadvantage gets reflected from the educational statistics which shows that gender disparity is more in SC category in comparison with other categories (Aggarwal & Sibou, 1994).

Apart from this, location and quality of institution affects the participation of students pursuing higher education. The geographical location of the institution is important especially for access of those residing in rural areas. From the NSSO figures, it becomes clear that Scheduled Caste student in rural areas lag behind even the Scheduled Tribes (Ghosh, 2008). This necessitates the need of having reservation for SC students on location basis as there is existing disparity within the category on such count (Premi, 1989). The fact of location is further reiterated by Agarwal (2009) who found that GER (Gross Enrolment Ratio) is lowest among rural poor at 1.3. In addition, the quality of institution is important as it is found that high quality of institution with limited strength of student makes environment for better survival of student in the system (Tinto, 1975).

But on academic count, the output in college is most significant for retention of a student in higher education (Reason, 2009) though it is being shaped of different external and internal factors (Tinto,

1975) of which some have been discussed in the previous lines. However there is low participation of SC students especially in technical institutions (Aikara, 1980; Report of the Commissioner for the Scheduled Castes and Scheduled Tribes, 1956; Premi, 1983; Sachidananda & Sinha, 1989). It is observed that the performance of SC students is rather average and below that of Non- Scheduled Caste/Tribe student (Kirpal et al, 1985). The result is most of the SC students in comparison with Non SC students, are stagnating or dropping out, therefore contributing to the lower academic output (Aikara, 1980).

The phenomenon of dropping out among SC students at higher education could be assigned to several factors prominently being high academic cost (Premi, 1989; Chakrabarti, 2009; Azam & Blom, 2008), their desperation for employment in the meanwhile (Aikara, 1980; Premi, 1989). The desperation for employment among the SC students could be explained through increased opportunity cost as one of the cause, which is the direct outcome of the increased globalization (Weisskopf, 2004). It is found that with the coming of Globalization, opportunity cost to have education for the deprived SC students has gone up as they could have gainful employment in lieu of getting education to have specialized skills which is much dearer now (Akhoury, 2008).

Disparity among SC Category in Higher Education

Regarding parity level in the SC category at higher education level, some of the studies have been conducted which can be placed as:

Chitnis (1981) points out that there is low enrolment of SC students in higher education as per the 1981 census. This is basically due to the reasons as getting employment in iii or iv grade jobs and due to their dismal participation and dropping out at earlier stages of education. It seems that major reason for such a scenario is their increasing opportunity cost due to their low economic background and also social stereotypical attitude which forces them to drop out. The situation becomes worse for the girl students.

It is also found by Aggarwal and Sibou (1994) who had conducted study on secondary enrolment data of SC students between 1964 and1977, that the gender disparity is more in SC category in comparison with other categories. This is due to economic reasons and household property.

Rationale of the Study

Most of the earlier related works (Chitnis, 1976, Aikara, 1980, Premi, 1983) have done their studies prior to the period of Liberalization, Privatization and Globalization in India (1991), or found several linkages of the disadvantaged status of SCs (Akhoury, 2008). Though Teltumbde in his article 'state, market and Dalits' has provided some theoretical underpinnings of the impact of the liberalized policies of the state on higher education of SCs, however display of the data showing trends of enrolment, shift in choices, the parity between SCs and General on one hand and that between the genders of the 'SC' community is left untouched. This study would shed light to this dimension. Views of Mehta & Kapur (2004) who have examined political economy of higher education in India seems to be oversimplified in nature and doesn't hint towards the problems of the marginalized in grabbing the benefits of getting higher education under the present system and how they would be suffering under privatization.

There are various studies which were conducted on participation of SCs in a single university or in single state as done by Gorettilourdes (2002), Chalam (1988), Velaskar (1986), Sinha (1989), etc. which did not mentioned about the enrolment situation of SCs in different states of India. Further there are various studies on financing of higher education in India and also which dealt about the issue of privatization in the same, however none of these studies are complete in discussing the issue of privatization in Indian higher education and also some of these studies did not made linkage with the equity issue in higher education. However various such related literatures are important base for the present study which tried to look the issue of privatization in Indian higher education and will try to link it with the enrolment trends of scheduled caste students in higher education in different states of India. Further the study has attempted to explore gender parity in higher education among the SC category.

METHODOLOGY

The broad purpose of the study was to analyze 'privatization' in Indian higher education by the way of government policies, programs, and plans. The study also tried to see the impact of privatization in higher education on Scheduled Caste (SC) student's enrolment. Further the study has taken an initiative to explore the gaps in terms of enrolment between SC and General Category students in higher education at various levels after initiation of liberalization policies in India i.e. after 1991. Apart from these, the study was having a motive to notice the trend for parity level among girls and boys of SC category in higher education at various levels.

Research Design

The present study was descriptive in nature. The study was conducted by using secondary data only. Secondary data were sourced from various documents such as U.G.C. Annual Report, Annual Report (MHRD), Selected Educational Statistics, and National Sample Survey Organisation for analyzing enrolment of SCs in higher education. To analyze the 'Privatization' in Indian higher education system on the ground of feasibility from the aspect of legal provisions, social equity, and political aspirations, critical review of various government policies on higher education and in various five year plans was done by the investigator. Information was also collected from various books, articles, research papers and unpublished dissertation and theses.

Collection of Data

As mentioned above this study was conducted by analyzing the data from secondary sources only. The objective of study was twofold, one is to study the phenomena of privatization in higher education and its impact on SC enrolment, and another is to see the enrolment trend among SCs.

Enrolment figures of SC students (both boys and girls) in higher education were collected for a period of fifteen years from 1991-92 to 2005-06 to see enrolment trend. The participation of SC students was not seen in isolation but was compared with the enrolment of General students in higher education to find out the difference in their representation in the higher education system. Therefore enrolment figures for general students were also collected for a period of fifteen years from 1991-92 to 2005-06. The enrolment trend between the SCs and general students was seen from various dimensions which included enrolment by region at various levels and in various courses. The enrolment figures of both SCs and general students were collected for all the states of India to assess the situation of SCs in higher education in different regions.

To analyze participation of SCs at various levels, enrolment figures were collected for different levels of higher education (i.e. Under Graduate, Post Graduate. M.Phil and Ph.D.). These enrolment figures were collected for various courses which included both general and professional courses. General courses here mean to enrolment in arts, science and commerce subjects while professional courses included medical, engineering and education.

The objective of analyzing privatization in higher education and its impact on SC students was fulfilled with both the secondary data from various sources and with the help of various policy analysis, and scholarly literature whose source was explored from different libraries as UGC, Nehru Memorial, JNU, NUEPA, etc. and from online database such as JSTOR. The investigator consulted reports of various commission and committees on higher education such as Kothari Commission, Radhakrishnan Commission, Ramamurti Committee, Punnaya Committee, Mahmoodchaman and Anankrishnan Committee, Birla Ambani Committee, and also CABE committee report. Apart from these, the researcher has consulted various policy documents consulted for the purpose of the study which comprises of National Policy on Education- 1968, 1986, Programme of Action-1992, and various Five Year Plans from First Five Year Plan to Tenth Five Year Plan. For the enrolment and participation of SC and General category students, an exhaustive glance has been made on Selected

Educational Statistics, various issues of Analysis of Budgeted Expenditure on Education, UGC Annual Report, Annual Report MHRD, and different year reports of SC/ST Commission.

Limitations of the Data

For the present study data utilized were only from the secondary sources as mentioned earlier in this chapter. There were various limitations in using such data as the data were not available for all the states in different years for various disciplines in higher education. Also, some of the error is quite obvious when the secondary data were utilized (Best & Kahn, 2006). Further, there are no distinct data available for the drop outs and for the repeaters in the institution(s). At the same time data are unavailable for number of enrolments of SC students in privately managed institutions. Apart from this the data for newly created states i.e. Uttarakhand, Chhattisgarh, and Jharkhand are available for the years after 2001 and therefore analyzing the trends in these states was not possible and therefore the data for these were added to their parent state i.e. U.P., M.P., and Bihar in the respective terms.

Statistical Tools Used

The secondary data of the study were analyzed utilizing the per centage for achieving the objective of calculating enrolment trends among SC students. And for the comparison of enrolment trends among SCs and General Category students, compound average growth has been calculated. The formula utilized for calculation of Compound Average Growth Rate is

$$\text{CAGR} = (\text{Ending Value} \div \text{Beginning Value})\ \hat{}\ (1 \div \text{No. of Years}) - 1$$

Finally, a parity level index is formulated for the comparison between girls and boys of SC category in higher education. The formula for calculation of parity level is

$$\text{Parity level} = \text{enrolment of Girls} \div \text{enrolment of boys}$$

3

Privatization of Higher Education

Policy Perspective

The aim of the present study was to explore 'privatization' in higher education in India from the social angle and also what impact it has made on the enrolment trend of the Scheduled Caste students in their higher education for which enrolment trends in different states of India has been analyzed for the period of fourteen years starting from 1991. The present chapter deals with the explanation of privatization of higher education in India. Such an explanation is attempted through analysis of various government policies which have bearing on the higher education of India. This is done in accordance with the first objective of the study.

Privatization in Higher Education in India

This section deals with Indian Governments policy towards Higher Education since independence impacting SC student's enrolment. Also it will analyze liberalization era in Indian Higher education system which paves way for privatization juxtapose to constitutional ideals of socialistic and democratic welfare state. Further to notice the liberal trends in Higher Education it becomes essential to evaluate the composition and share of Higher Education in Various five year plans.

Importance of Higher Education for the state's development has been recognized during pre-independence struggle and was emphasized accordingly by the then national leaders. Higher

Education was rightly placed under state's surveillance after independence as a component of various welfare activities undertaken by the state of India. The notion of welfare state came into being only after the end of 2nd world war when it was realized that role of state was to further welfare forms apart fulfilling its basic duty to provide protection. And education was considered as an important agent to promote welfare in the state due to various externalities attached to it. Therefore it was supposed to be a state's responsibility to provide education to larger number of people residing in the state. In this context, Higher Education needs special attention in the developing nation like India, where it has too much social returns (11 per cent) attached to it (Tilak, 2008) apart from its contribution to economic growth essential for developed status (Verghese, 2001; Sadlak, 1998). The importance of subsidization of Higher Education by the state to achieve greater development by democratizing the same has been realized by Keynesian model (Halsey, 1997). Further it is a well recognized fact that education as a whole is the most important tool to produce 'human capital' making human resource an asset instead of a liability over the state. However, such potent tool does not turn out to be a complete panacea for all existing ills, particularly it did not help much to dilute the existent social hierarchies and reproduce the social hierarchy and privilege(s) (Bowles & Gintis, 1976). This has necessitated Indian law makers to establish provisions for reservation to ensure adequate participation from the deprived as well as from discriminated sections i.e. from the communities of OBC's, ST's and SC's (Constitution of India) and participation of various such groups particularly SC's in education has shown a resultant increase in there status (Chaterjee, 2000), therefore reservation policy as mentioned in the Constitution of India is an essential requirement to have more inclusiveness which is required to have real development in the state (Thorat, 2004).

This Policy of affirmative action becomes much more crucial in the wake of scenario when parity of SC students in comparison to unreserved students is far from achievement particularly at higher education level where there GER is 6.30 per cent while it is 16.60

for unreserved category. Further the policy of liberalization in higher education has affected adversely for all students (Tilak, 1997) who are deprived on economic grounds and therefore is likely to affect negatively the SC students who are economically deprived and socially discriminated (Teltumbde, 2008).

State Policy for Education since Independence

This section makes analysis of Indian government's policy towards higher education by looking at various committees/commissions report which was set up exclusively for education and also by looking towards various educational policies announced so far. The analysis here is done keeping privatization and development of SC in prime focus. After independence India's education policy had shifted in terms of a goal attached to it. Previously education was designed to consolidate the base of colonial power (Britain) while since independence the education was designed to suit the national aspirations (Sarkar, 1983). Nehru's remarks to the educational conference of 1948 strongly expressed the view[1] that

> "Whenever conferences were called to form a plan for education in India, the tendency as a rule, was to maintain the existing system with slight modification. This must not happen now. Great changes have taken place in the country and the education system must also be in keeping view with them. The entire basis of education must be revolutionized."

The national goals which education would be promoting were documented in the constitution of India as promotion of democracy, secularism, socialist society to create national integration (Naik, 1965).

Radhakrishnan Commission

This was the first commission set up in independent India to introspect higher education India under the chairmanship of

Dr. S. Radhakrishnan in 1948. This commission has recommended reconstruction of University education, after realizing its importance for future development of India in varied terms (Kamat, 1989), to meet the demand for socio- economic development via strengthening of scientific, technical and other human power. Major recommendations of Radhakrishnan Commission can be summed up as –

a. Emphasis on student's welfare by way of providing scholarship, stipend, hostel, library and medical facilities.
b. Learning of three languages i.e. regional, federal and English.
c. Establishment of rural universities to have comprehensive development of nation.
d. Universities to be an autonomous unit.
e. University education to be kept in concurrent list.
f. Expansion of women's education.

The report stands for the establishment of egalitarian society and thus mentions—

> "Education is a universal right and not a class privilege.....in distribution of educational opportunity there should be no caprice, prejudice, favouritism special privilege or other arbitrary action. In general each person should have the educational opportunities on the kind and extent, which represent the fair share of the total educational resources" (GoI, 1962: 500-51)

In sum it can be said that this commission had a vision of having socio economic development and social capitalism by university education and therefore thinks higher education as an obligation of the state while keeping academic autonomy. So on financial grounds Radhakrishnan commission suggested states responsibility to aid and support higher education.

Establishment of University Grants Commission (UGC)

Favouring state's responsibility to provide higher education Radhakrishnan Comission had suggested for establishment of UGC. As a result in 1950 the Ministry of Education prepared a raft bill entitled "the Universities (Regulation of Standards) Bill"[2] with an objective to have a central governing authority to control establishment and standards of University (ies) in the country. This bill was discarded due to various contentions by different established universities of the state on grounds of autonomy. However, UGC was eventually established in 1953 and worked as an ad-hoc agency till 1956 when it got statutory standing (Singh, 1981). The role of UGC during the succeeding years can however be doubted as it did not play an independent professional role (as was assigned) and succumbed to economic and political forces which has hampered the appropriate development of higher education in terms of quality and quantity (Singh, 1981).

Kothari Commission (1964-1966)

The most important document of education India is Kothari Commission's report. This commission was set up in 1964 under the chairmanship of Dr.D.S.Kothari, the then chairman of UGC, to guide government on various facets of education system to improve it further by transforming it. Its report entitled as 'Education and National Development' mentions that "if .... 'Change on grand scale has to be achieved without violent revolution ... there is one instrument i.e. Education' (GOI 1966:4) and clears that revolution in education can revolutionize the entire socio – economic and cultural growth (Power, 1995:39). Major recommendation s of the report which deals with higher education, its financing, and equity issues can be stated as

a. Establishment of 'Major Universities 'to achieve goal of improved quality and standard of higher education.
b. Expansion of quality higher educational institutions.

c. To reduce inequalities in higher education, it recommended scholarship programmes, hostel accommodations for rural students etc. to mobilize students for weaker sections.
d. Expansion of free ships and scholarships to have more inclusive higher education.
e. It strictly mentions the state funding of higher education' however, philanthropic efforts may continue.
f. There can be private assistance to government in producing quality higher education but in long term government control should become full.
g. The education at all levels should be free and it is the state's responsibility to ensure it. For achievement of such a goal the commission recommends for expenditure by government share which should not be less than 6 per cent of the GDP (Gross Domestic Product).

National Policy on Education (NPE) 1968

Various recommendations made by Kothari Commission were not accepted by the Government of India due to various reasons as immature socio-political environment was existent during that period which made states to contest the suggestions (Kamat, 1989) and also due to various flaws in it leading to failure in development of comprehensive policy statement (Naik, 1982). However the first comprehensive plan was developed in India in the form of National Policy on Education 1968 carrying various recommendations by Kothari Commission. Regarding Higher Education as mentioned by the Kothari Commission, NPE' 68 suggests for

a. Expansion of higher education.
b. State to have complete authority to establish higher educational institutions in the country.
c. There should be efforts to equalize educational opportunities with special emphasis to develop education among backward classes.

National Policy on Education (NPE) 1986

After more than one and a half decade of NPE'68, it was an effort to revisit and reformulate education policy of the nation and the result came out in the form of another National Policy on Education in 1986. Placing importance of Higher Education, the policy states that

> "Higher education provides people with an opportunity to reflect on the critical social, economic, cultural, moral and spiritual issues facing humanity. It contributes to national development through dissemination of specialized knowledge and skills" (GOI, 1986).

Major recommendations of NPE'86 in regard to higher education its funding and development of SC's in higher education can be placed as

a. Expansion of higher education considering efficiency in utilization of available resources.
b. To coordinate with the expansion and quality maintenance of the higher education system in the states, a national apex body at the central government level and state councils of higher education at the state levels were proposed.(GOI, 1986).
c. In the name of efficiency and effectiveness, it has recommended private role in higher professional education, however the role has to be determined by the state. So that there remains no scope for commercialization (GOI, 1986).
d. Regarding finances and resources, the policy mentions for the raising of fees to have more sense of responsibility among the stake holders. However, at the same time the policy reiterates the share of education to be kept at 6 per cent of GDP or more (GOI, 1986).
e. Higher education to be job oriented.
f. It recommends tom set up rural universities such that rural students do not remain deprived.

g. Regarding SC's the policy has declared for special emphasis for the education of SC's at all levels. However, it mentions only provisions for their education at primary and secondary level such as initiatives to their families, pre-matric scholarships, hostel facilities etc.(GOI, 1986)

Ramamurti Committee (1990)

The National Policy on Education of 1986 was reviewed by a committee set up under chairmanship of Acharya Ramamurti in 1990. The committee prepared a report entitled "*Towards a Just and Humane Society*" which gave its recommendations on the basis of review of NPE'86. Various important components of the report with specific references to financial consideration and participation of SC's in higher education can be summarized as-

a. It emphasized quality improvement in higher educational institutions and for this suggested to link up higher education with people's initiatives and local planning (GoI, 1990).
b. There was suggestion for opening rural universities by providing them autonomy to boost talent at the grassroot level (GoI, 1990)
c. It had suggested a plan to set up National Council for Higher Education (GOI, 1990).
d. There should be planned growth of higher education under the effective control of UGC to have efficient utilization of the available resources and less burden on state government.
e. Regarding the resource and financial burden. It has recommended for enhancing the tuition as well a other fees to recover the cost and reduce the burden on state government. However the enhancement is to be made according to income level of the family of the student.
f. The committee fails to take into consideration the social discrimination prevalent in Indian society and therefore the socially excluded caste i.e. scheduled caste remained

so in the policy report in terms of their participation in higher education.

g. The committee is having favourable opinion about liberation of higher and incorporation of elements like loan, finance by nationalized banks and other institutions, especially for the technical and management educational institutes making them financially self dependent.

Cabinet Advisory Board on Education (CABE) on 1992 has reviewed Radhakrishnan Committee report to formulate a revised educational document in the name of Programme of Action (POA). CABE committee report reiterated policy framework of NPE'86 thinking that as adequate for the time. However it has rejected the proposal to set up statutory for higher education to check unplanned growth. Major recommendation was for providing financial autonomy to various institutes of higher learning with various solutions as educational loan and other such financial assistance by banks, etc.

Programme of Action 1992

On the basis of reports of CABE committee and Ramamurthy Committee Programme of Action was prepared in 1992.it has mentioned various proposals of which major proposals are in reference to higher education, its financing and SC's development can be stated as –

1. It recommended to set up state council of higher education on the guidelines maintained by UGC (GOI, 1992)
2. It proposed for expansion of higher educational institutions, however funding is major area of concern for which it made provision for enhancement of tuition fees.
3. Recommendations made by the Gnanam committee with regard to changes in the management structure of the universities should be implemented by all states as and when approved by CABE.

4. The government should exercise restrain in setting up more central universities.
5. Establishment of autonomous departments and units to decentralize administrative, academic and financial powers in universities.
6. Setting up Central Council of Rural Institutes (GoI, 1992).
7. The technical and management institutes will be encouraged to generate there own resources by way of enhanced fees, consultancy and testing services, donations etc. (GoI, 1992).
8. Private and voluntary effort in technical education will be encouraged within the framework of guidelines and norms prescribed by AICTE.
9. Regarding Scheduled Caste students POA speaks lot about enrolment retention and participation of scheduled caste students in primary and secondary education with various incentives as scholarships, books, hostels etc. along with coaching remedial classes and adult education for these communities. However, there is no conspicuous mentor of their participation n higher education.

Other Committees and Reports

Punnaya Committee

This committee was set up by UGC in 1992-93 which suggested that universities should generate 15 per cent of its annual maintenance expenditure through internally generated resources and this should go up to at least 25 per cent at the end of 10 years. This committee also recommended that students receiving higher education should bear a reasonable proportion of the cost of higher education.

Dr. Swaminathan Panel 1992

It was set up by AICTE to have financial recommendations for technical education. Broadly it placed the idea of collecting educational-cess from industries and other organizations to promote technical education.

Mahmood Chaman committee and Anandkrishnan Committee

These committees were set up to review the fee structure in Delhi University. They have made recommendations which indicated that the total financial burden of education would have to be borne by parents and private sector would enter the field of higher education (Agarwal and Sharma:2004)

Birla Ambani Report 2000

In 2000, industrialists Kumar Mangalam Birla and Mukesh Ambani prepared a report after introduction of Private University Bill in the same year some of the major suggestions made in the report are-

a. Government should confine itself to primary education and higher education should be provided by the private sector.
b. Passage of the Private University Bill.
c. Enforcement of the User Pay principle in higher education.
d. Loans and grants to the economically weaker sections of the society.

3.3 Financing of Higher Education in India since Independence

Funding or financing of higher education in India has always remained a core issue of the debate among scholars and also among policy makers. After independence as importance for higher education for national development was recognized, it was made clear in the policies there on to have funding of higher education through state. Hence, the government has provided the support both for development and maintenance of higher education in India by the means of colleges and universities. However this trend of financial support by the state government got transformed with development of different governing policies and finally there has been almost exponential growth of private unaided colleges and universities which gets support from self financing programmes. This shift of higher education towards financial liberalization where market determines the price is reflected in declining share of education in various five year plans and also in various government allotments towards higher education in a financial year as compared to elementary education which is supposed to be asocial good while the former is considered as private good (as has been mentioned by world bank).

Trends of Financing Higher Education in India

Financing is a major factor that helps getting the anticipated outcome for any plan irrespective of sector of economy of the state. In India, we can witness two distinct phases in financing of higher education i.e. pre 1980 and period after that. This is reflected in National Policy of Education 1986 which gave clarion call to reduce financial burden of the state to support education sector as a whole and higher education particularly (NPE'1986). However such policy got implemented in heart and soul with initialization of liberal policies since 1991 as an influence of policies of globalization. This has paved way for 'privatization' in higher education leading to reduction in government's share, in over all expenditure from 80 per cent in 1983 to 67 per cent in 1999, and increase in private expenditure on the other side. Also, it resulted in acceleration of private institutions since 1990s (Agarwal, 2007).

Prior to 1980s the state was the dominant actor in dispensing and controlling higher education in India and majority of the higher educational institutions were under direct control of the state. However, after the guidelines mentioned in National Policy of Education 1986, government has provided support to private colleges established by various societies, trusts, etc. and therefore number of aided institutions have risen and also there has been initiative by government to promote more number of self financing courses shifting incidence of bearing higher education on the students or their family. And recently phenomenon of 'Deemed University', 'Unaided' private colleges, etc. symbolizing privatization, has come in the scenario in more strengthened way (Sharma, 2000). The trend of decreasing public share and increase in that of private sector can be noted down from the figures provided by Anandakrishnan in 2006 where share of unaided higher educational have increased from 42.6 in 2000 to 63.21 per cent in 2005. Such initiative can be regarded as an attempt towards "direct" privatization in higher education (Tilak, 2002) where unrestricted private institutions are invited to impart higher education.

It was Kothari Commission (1964-66) who firstly recommended 6 per cent as a government's share for education sector as a whole out of the total GDP of the state. And such recommendation has remained an 'ideal' for the policies formulated thereafter which have reiterated the same per cent share in their guidelines but is still a dream as during the entire period since than the government's share on an average is around 3 per cent (Sharma, 2000).

Since 1991 when the period of liberalization has begun in India on extensive scale with LPG (Liberalization, Privatization, Globalization) policies in every sector, share of public expenditure on higher education has declined in real terms with annual growth rate of 5.4 per cent however at current prices the annual growth rate is 12.3 per cent (Prakash, 2007). Annual expenditure of government on higher education was 13.2 and 4.8 per cent for university and other Higher Education, and for technical education respectively in 1991 which have reduced to 11.66 and 3.87 per cent in respective terms in 2005. (see Table 3.1).

By analyzing various Five Year Plans announced by Planning Commission in India, it becomes quite evident that there was increase in priority for higher education as from 8 in the first plan the per cent expenditure for higher education has increased to 28 per cent in the Fifth Plan except marginal reduction of 3 per cent in third Five Year Plan. However since Fifth Plan, there is continuous fall in share expenditure towards education at higher

Table 3.1: Annual Expenditure of Government on Education

Annual Expenditure of Government on Higher Education		
Years	*University & other Higher Education*	*Technical Education*
1991 (B E)	13.2	4.8
1992	12.89	4.33
1993	13.26	4.35
1994	12.95	4.37
1995	12.28	4.09
1996	11.79	3.99
1997	11.82	3.95
1998	11.94	4.05
1999	13.46	4.01
2000	14.71	4.04
2001	12.47	3.95
2002 (B E)	12.56	4
2003	12.4	3.99
2004	11.69	3.87
2005	11.66	3.87

Source: Analysis of Budgeted Expenditure on Education, MHRD.

level and the share has reached to 6 per cent in 10th plan after steep fall of 10 per cent from seventh Five Year Plan. (see Table 3.2 and Figure 3.1).

Apart from the total expenditure, government's expenditure on scholarship awarded to the students pursuing higher education has reduced after the period of liberalization has begun in India (since 1991).

As evident from the Table 3.1, the amount spent on higher education in general and for technical education scholarships, has increased from Rs. 113 million in 1990 to Rs. 183 million in 2004 at current prices for higher education, and for technical education from Rs. 20 million to Rs. 36 million for period from 1990 to 2004. However the per cent share on amount spent on scholarship out of total expenditure on higher education has declined from 0.62 for general higher education and 0.45 for technical education in 1990 to 0.24 and 0.2 per cent for higher and technical education respectively (Prakash, 2007).

After the recommendation of National Policy of Education 1986 and Programme of Action 1992, the efforts have been initiated

Table 3.2: Per cent Plan Expenditure on University and Higher Education

Five Year Plan period	*Percent Plan Expenditure*
I	8
II	18
III	15
IV	25
V	28
VI	21
VII	16
VIII	10
IX	9
X	6

Source: Various Five Year Plans, Government of India.

by the government of India to reduce its share to bear higher education in the state and to search for alternative sources to fund higher education. Various options that were looked at, included privatization, increased cost of higher education, cost recovery schemes as loan, credit market, etc. The first indication of government's policy change is visible from the recommendations made in the Eighth Five Year Plan (1992-97) which stated that the opening of new conventional universities and colleges should not be encouraged and there should be promotion of more voluntary organizations and agencies to open institutions for higher learning and make it self financing (Azad, 2001). (see Table 3.3).

In 1992, Justice Punnaya Committee was appointed to recommend about financing of higher education in central as well as other institutions. The committee report has emphasized role of higher education in social mobility and therefore state's intervention is required. However, such recommendations remained there in the papers, and in the name of state's financial support for higher education UGC in 1995 issued a directive to all the universities that the funds allocated for education in general and higher education in particular will be subjected to the broad parameters of economic reforms and market liberalization (Anand & Sharma, 2004).

As a further step towards privatization of financing of higher education in India, Ministry of Finance's Paper on government

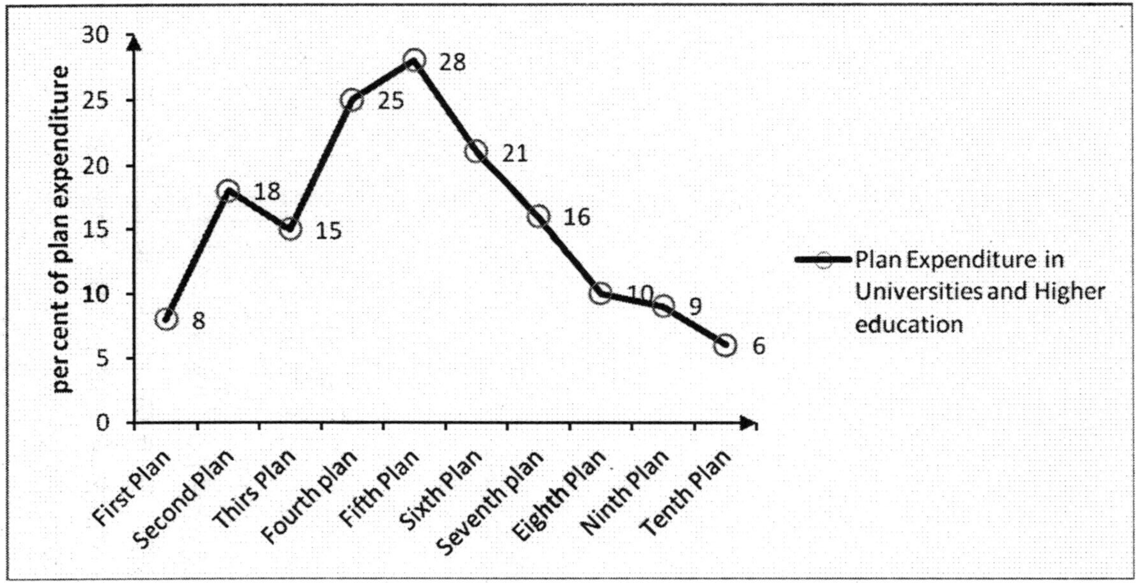

Figure 3.1: Plan Expenditure on Higher Education as % of Total Plan Expenditure

Source: Annual Financial Statistics of Education Sector 2003-04, MHRD, Govt. of India, New Delhi, 2005.5.

Table 3.3: Expenditure on Scholarships in Higher and Technical Education

Year	*Higher Education*		*Technical Education*	
	Rs. in Million (Current Prices)	*Percentage to Total Expenditure on Higher Education*	*Rs. in Million (Current Prices)*	*Percentage to Total Expenditure on Technical Education*
1990-91	113	0.62	20	0.45
1001-92	I30	0.67	24	0.48
1992-03	126	0.57	21	0.37
1993-94	134	0.47	57	0.94
1994-95	140	0.44	19	0.26
1995-96	147	0.41	18	0.23
1996-97	171	0.44	63	0.63
1997-98	134	0.3	19	0.19
1998-99	203	0.34	21	0.17
1999-2000	190	0.27	17	0.12
2000-01	153	0.24	36	0.25
2001-02	116	0.16	36	0.28
2002-03	115	0.16	77	0.53
2003-04 RE	191	0.25	71	0.43
2004-05 BE	183	0.24	36	0.2

Source: Analysis of Budgeted Expenditure on Education. MHRD; RE—revenue Expenditure, BE—Budgeted Expenditure

subsidies titled as "Government Subsidies in India: A Discussion Paper" came in 1997. It declared higher education as a 'non-merit' good leaving it to students or consumers to finance it (Azad, 2004). This was the direct influence of recommendations by World Bank in 1995 which declared less government fund for higher education and increased privatization for the same. In continuation to this, efforts towards financial privatization of higher education has been strengthened by initiating a Private University Bill in 1995 and further a Committee was constituted under chairmanship of two industrialists (Kumarmangalam Birla and Mukesh Ambani) in 2001 which recommended for total abstain of government form higher education. Though the Bill for Private University of 1995 did not get passed and also Ambani Birla Report did not got approval in the parliament, it is not a complete respite for the proponents of equity, both social as well as economical, as the state policy has clandestinely supported the liberalization, privatization and Globalization making state to reduce its share to finance higher education.

Having a glance at the state's policy towards higher education in India and the financing trends of the same from 1947 till the present time, it becomes quite emphatic that the State's policies are having a direct bearing on the financial allocation towards higher education in different plans, programs and budgets. Since 1947, the state policy towards higher education has been favourable and therefore higher education was placed under state domain. This policy of state protection is reflected in various commission's reports as Radha Krishnan Commission, Kothari Commission, and in National Policy of Education in 1968 where the importance of higher education was acknowledged and therefore have recommended for higher allocation of funds (at least 6 per cent) out of total share of GDP. Such a policy with constitutional obligation of providing adequate reservation to the deprived section(s) albeit not implemented in soul even, has continued till 1980 which is a watershed year in enhancing private participation in Indian higher education sector (Agarwal, 2007). After 1980s, there has been shift towards liberalization of higher education in terms of encouragement towards private players. This is clearly visible in the National Policy of Education in 1986 and also in subsequent policies and reports which conspicuously suggests for reducing the state's burden to support higher education (NPE '86, PoA '92, Ramamurti Committee Report (1992), Punnaya Committee Report (1992)). Implication of such policies got reflected in proliferation of private institutions offering higher education (mainly professional education) and also in decline in government's share for higher education since Seventh Five Year Plan (Table 3.2).

After 7th Plan, there has been tremendous rise in capitation fee charging colleges, particularly in professional courses (Azad: 2004). Further there has been increase in number of self-financing colleges/courses which has exorbitant fee structure (Azad, 2004). The catalyst in such a change is the phenomenon of 'globalization' where education is included in General Agreement on Trade and Services (1995) and higher education is recognized as 'non-merit' good. Thereafter, large number of private unaided colleges has mushroomed on Indian higher education scenario (Anand Krishnan, 2006). This will turn higher education costly (Pawar, 2002) and a gross negative impact will be marked on enrolment and participation of students in general and will be a disaster for the constitutional commitment to establish equity in the state providing positive discrimination to the deprived through reservation policy. And the GER for India in higher education; which is low at around 11 per cent, when the developed nations are having GER more than 50 per cent, may experience a negative trend or concentrated participation of economically well off students, if institutes which are purely private entities with their own products (own cause, syllabus, structure, fees, etc.) gets established all over the country (Chalam, 2004). In terms of financial or economic efficiency, the ground which is promoted to favour privatization, it is interesting to note down that even if complete privatization is allowed in higher education it will have marginal impact on fiscal deficit of the state (Narayana, 2006) while it will majorly impact in adverse terms for enrolment of poor (social and economic) background students.

Further it has been identified that if the prevailing 'black economy' in the country which is having a share of 40 per cent of GDP is trapped, (Kumar, 2004) then there will be enough liquid (in terms of money) to support entire higher education system along with tackling other fiscal challenges.

3.4 Conclusion

In India, at the time of independence, higher education was thought to be of significant importance and therefore investment in furthering the same in the country was made by the state albeit private players were allowed in the system in conjunction with the former.

Various policies, plans and programs that were formulated in India for higher education got reflection of State's dominance in controlling the higher education. However, such dominance withered away with the initiative of liberalization era giving way for the private players to share the financial burden to bear the expense of higher education in the country. This was reflected firstly in NPE '86 where it was clearly recommended to look for alternatives to fund higher education. This has negatively impacted the enrolment of all the students whose GER declined from 12.4 per cent in 2001 to 11.55 per cent in 2005. This was the first attempt to sacrifice equity to gain surmised economic efficiency as in the long term, real economic as well as social development will take place in proportion of knowledge society a state is having. In this policy of education, no clear mention for the participation of SCs in higher education was made which was followed in the policies thereafter.

Privatization in higher education was made extensive after 1990s under the influence of 'globalization' and world politics where higher education was understood as 'private good' yielding private benefits and therefore incidence of having it should be directly placed on its consumer i.e. student or family (Tilak, 1997). Along with this, the government's share and support to higher education has reduced (Agarwal, 2006). This has led to increased share of private players which can be categorized as (Chalam, 2004).

(a) Institutions that receive grant from the government, but the management is done by private people.
(b) Institutions that charge fees and offer approved syllabus of the government through university structures.
(c) Institutions that are purely private commercial entities with their own products (own course, fees and content) with foreign collaboration or with franchise to market products in India market.

Among these, the last category institution which are unrestricted, poses the major threat to 'inclusiveness', equity and will further private interests in terms of profit, and content, etc.

Notes

1. see Sujit Kumar Choudhary (2008), Higher Education in India: A Socio Historical Journey from Ancient to 2006-7, *Journal of Educational Enquiry*, vol. 8, no. 1, 2008, pp. 50-72.
2. See Amrik Singh, Foundation and Role of UGC, *Journal of Higher Education* Vol. 7, No. 1 Monsoon 1981, UGC, New Delhi.

4

Enrolment Trends among Scheduled Caste Students in Higher Education

Following various policies with the content of liberalizing ideology as a rule, education didn't emerge as an exception to it. Though the elementary education is declared as 'Merit' good, its delivery mechanism is not designed meticulously and therefore anticipated results were spared. Its implication is very much significant for the achievement of higher education level by the students. However our prime concern for this chapter is about the enrolment trends among the scheduled caste student in higher education (particularly). Such an analysis holds importance for the reason of having estimation of the gravity of the situation which may likely to get worsen if the state's support is withdrawn (from their higher education) to facilitate private players.

The present chapter highlights the enrolment trends of Scheduled Caste students in higher education at various levels in different streams since 1991 till 2005. These trends are analyzed for all the states of India except few where the related data were not available. Also, the growth trend of Scheduled Caste students and that of unreserved category in different levels and disciplines is being analyzed for the said period with a break at 1997 the year from which we can notice more number of private aided and unaided institutions offering self financing courses a way towards full privatization. Apart for the enrolment and growth trends, chapter will deal with the parity level existing in Scheduled Caste category for higher level of learning and it is compared with parity level in unreserved category. (see Table 4.1)

Table 4.1: Percent Share of SCs in various courses

State				A P	Assam	Bihar	Goa	Gujarat	Haryana	H P	J & K	Karnataka	Kerala	MP	Maharashtra
1991	GenEdn	UG	B	12.33	7.83	0.00	0.63	8.73	8.75	8.20	3.35	14.86	8.70	9.24	13.06
			G	9.59	7.41	0.00	0.33	5.50	1.93	3.86	1.40	7.00	7.98	3.98	7.32
			T	11.47	7.70	0.00	0.48	7.34	6.39	6.82	2.61	11.98	8.31	7.72	16.15
		PG	B	15.99	6.19	0.00	0.91	11.84	8.93	15.55	8.29	0.00	12.52	8.24	13.79
			G	11.15	4.70	0.00	0.50	7.25	2.48	4.52	3.01	0.00	7.67	4.10	8.26
			T	14.84	5.59	0.00	0.72	9.92	6.03	11.37	5.74	0.00	9.67	6.87	12.23
		Ph.D	B	4.14	1.33	NA	NA	2.35	0.76	5.89	2.14	NA	1.22	1.43	4.03
			G	4.64	0.00	NA	NA	1.11	0.46	2.96	0.50	NA	0.63	1.00	4.03
			T	4.25	0.83	NA	NA	1.92	0.62	4.75	1.38	NA	0.95	1.26	4.03
	ProfEdn	Eng	B	9.30	5.59	NA	2.00	4.24	15.45	14.36	5.99	4.21	8.39	10.17	NA
			G	7.49	6.40	NA	1.26	1.33	5.93	0.00	8.70	5.08	7.90	7.14	NA
			T	9.17	5.64	NA	1.83	3.93	14.50	13.11	6.11	4.27	8.27	9.91	NA
		Med	B	13.65	6.37	NA	3.62	9.30	16.87	14.56	5.93	1.77	6.66	11.66	11.36
			G	11.04	6.60	NA	6.77	6.82	8.67	9.88	6.33	2.24	9.85	7.70	8.82
			T	12.70	6.44	NA	5.17	8.46	13.91	13.45	6.09	1.89	7.82	10.45	10.24
		Edn	B	16.40	17.10	NA	NA	11.40	10.75	3.42	3.04	7.08	13.39	12.13	14.70
			G	6.94	3.86	NA	NA	6.41	3.92	3.03	2.66	3.30	8.59	2.93	6.13
			T	12.34	13.11	NA	NA	9.38	7.42	3.35	2.86	5.62	10.12	8.04	11.02
2001	GenEdn	UG	B	15.34	9.05	5.22	0.86	25.83	10.61	12.96	0.00	19.47	10.08	8.33	11.74
			G	11.95	8.55	1.42	0.60	6.27	5.54	9.95	0.00	6.37	9.06	7.49	8.47
			T	14.04	8.87	4.23	0.70	16.84	8.48	11.64	0.00	13.79	9.43	8.02	10.36

State				A P	Assam	Bihar	Goa	Gujarat	Haryana	H P	J & K	Karnataka	Kerala	MP	Maharashtra
		PG	B	14.57	8.25	0.99	2.60	12.25	19.63	18.73	0.00	23.75	14.56	10.97	18.61
			G	10.68	7.32	2.45	2.23	8.96	8.23	10.18	0.00	10.49	12.49	14.57	14.83
			T	13.20	7.89	1.13	2.34	10.59	13.39	14.64	0.00	20.45	13.14	12.30	17.28
		Ph.D	B	14.13	3.52	16.21	8.33	8.32	17.52	10.58	0.00	18.17	31.22	0.29	4.77
			G	8.87	3.14	16.55	4.55	7.29	6.14	5.35	0.00	14.52	56.30	0.61	2.37
			T	12.87	3.36	16.30	6.35	7.94	12.76	8.61	0.00	17.46	40.00	0.41	4.03
	ProfEdn	Eng	B	13.41	10.47	7.65	1.22	6.61	4.01	13.30	0.00	5.38	7.12	7.02	0.00
			G	12.01	23.92	5.80	1.02	5.69	2.53	15.85	0.00	6.65	8.30	2.37	0.00
			T	12.98	11.60	7.50	1.17	6.44	3.74	13.67	0.00	5.70	7.55	5.30	0.00
		Med	B	13.34	7.78	15.55	1.66	5.74	14.02	12.74	0.00	7.49	7.44	11.73	11.39
			G	15.03	6.73	15.49	1.40	4.72	7.52	6.38	0.00	9.46	10.34	12.24	11.20
			T	14.13	7.45	15.54	1.48	5.35	12.26	10.13	0.00	8.14	9.11	11.92	11.30
		Edn	B	14.99	13.32	16.25	4.00	11.88	18.60	14.66	0.00	14.51	14.34	14.09	13.01
			G	9.05	8.76	5.55	0.57	9.13	14.00	13.51	0.00	9.75	10.03	6.52	11.81
			T	12.66	11.52	10.90	1.01	10.67	15.88	14.36	0.00	12.68	11.10	11.29	12.65
2005	GenEdn	UG	B	16.53	5.46	10.22	1.62	8.62	11.76	11.25	5.26	16.42	15.13	21.38	14.50
			G	14.88	5.65	3.73	1.08	5.84	7.74	10.08	6.97	11.42	14.08	15.57	12.64
			T	15.94	5.52	8.60	1.28	7.34	9.77	10.69	5.95	14.04	14.44	18.56	13.64
		PG	B	14.70	6.74	12.79	3.14	10.69	14.52	15.09	5.07	19.11	14.53	24.46	16.34
			G	15.11	6.14	11.53	0.97	8.76	7.64	11.60	3.83	8.42	11.71	15.42	10.50
			T	14.85	6.49	12.59	1.68	9.62	10.77	13.16	4.36	13.02	12.43	19.47	13.38

State				A P	Assam	Bihar	Goa	Gujarat	Haryana	H P	J & K	Karnataka	Kerala	MP	Maharashtra
		Ph.D	B	12.74	0.36	11.46	0.00	5.31	10.17	10.96	7.47	12.59	3.95	31.47	6.74
			G	13.15	3.07	5.92	0.00	7.73	5.58	9.98	7.66	16.31	4.35	18.91	3.18
			T	12.84	1.37	9.41	0.00	6.07	8.21	10.54	7.56	13.78	4.14	25.99	5.49
	ProfEdn	Eng	B	11.91	12.33	16.21	1.20	8.89	4.18	10.08	3.08	5.73	8.41	13.57	5.65
			G	7.94	20.18	4.82	1.07	4.32	2.34	10.59	0.97	12.64	22.41	9.95	6.04
			T	10.73	13.87	12.57	1.15	7.61	3.75	10.17	2.17	7.36	13.71	12.41	5.74
		Med	B	23.95	9.14	11.98	2.95	5.71	16.31	15.89	26.57	16.13	9.85	20.69	9.99
			G	13.69	4.87	11.94	1.55	6.21	13.01	9.95	21.74	16.28	9.77	22.39	10.36
			T	18.66	7.65	11.97	2.00	5.90	14.83	12.95	24.01	16.20	9.80	21.37	10.17
		Edn	B	16.86	4.91	16.44	8.33	12.75	18.65	15.86	4.43	11.09	12.77	27.61	12.91
			G	14.12	6.99	2.90	1.14	11.92	11.02	11.16	7.42	11.71	14.11	18.43	17.39
			T	15.62	5.99	14.24	2.00	12.37	14.31	13.08	5.71	11.35	13.85	22.83	14.61

Table 4.1 (Contd.)

State				Orissa	Punjab	Rajasthan	TN	U P	W B	Chandigarh	Delhi	Pondicherry	India
1991	GenEdn	UG	B	7.257	14.02	9.6304	16.18	15.39	9.225	2.984	6.058	10.96	9.688
			G	3.966	7.617	1.5714	10.02	3.482	6.118	1.501	4.761	4.295	5.85
			T	6.405	10.6	7.6342	13.57	12.6	7.931	2.284	5.513	7.913	8.395
		PG	B	5.875	14.48	13.87	15.91	15.11	4.776	13.47	8.106	12.9	11.13
			G	3.826	6.039	1.6022	9.47	3.477	2.7	4.14	4.293	3.086	5.118

State				Orissa	Punjab	Rajasthan	TN	U P	W B	Chandigarh	Delhi	Pondicherry	India
			T	5.261	9.498	10.633	13.39	11.95	3.905	8.05	6.166	7.343	9.182
		Ph.D	B	5.66	3.438	5.5556	3.571	4.835	4.128	NA	3.08	NA	3.487
			G	5.556	1.617	1.5385	2.041	1.71	4.623	NA	1.674	NA	2.021
			T	5.638	2.43	3.871	3.106	4.019	4.287	NA	2.567	NA	3.002
	ProfEdn	Eng	B	9.113	16.06	NA	NA	0.627	4.388	15.24	11.39	13.73	5.581
			G	5.263	6.599	NA	NA	0.583	3.038	0.468	8.642	15.03	5.057
			T	8.97	15.23	NA	NA	0.625	4.319	9.272	11.11	14.07	5.536
		Med	B	9.83	25.62	NA	16.39	2.99	11.13	NA	10.94	15.27	8.764
			G	9.074	15	NA	14.86	1.382	3.653	NA	12.05	32.32	8.216
			T	9.61	20.82	NA	15.71	2.619	9.231	NA	11.44	18.33	8.574
		Edn	B	13.92	23.75	NA	21.35	13.57	9.363	47.73	6.545	20.59	11.65
			G	15.19	7.851	NA	15.19	3.603	0.997	10.76	9.851	15.12	5.071
			T	14.29	12.22	NA	17.41	9.225	5.545	14.14	8.733	16.67	8.67
2001	GenEdn	UG	B	9.04	10.51	12.665	22.24	17.3	14.58	8.473	10.19	17.86	13.99
			G	5.671	9.29	3.8521	16.02	7.513	7.891	5.103	7.018	11.46	8.178
			T	7.874	9.86	9.8084	19.26	13.56	11.34	6.618	8.539	13.87	11.57
		PG	B	7.871	11.6	16.595	21.19	18.05	25	13.31	11.04	28.01	14
			G	5.486	6.528	4.2166	14.27	8.093	12.24	5.88	5.383	10.49	9.724
			T	6.895	7.964	12.144	17.89	13.73	18.53	8.607	8.132	17.87	12.28

State				Orissa	Punjab	Rajasthan	TN	U P	W B	Chandigarh	Delhi	Pondicherry	India
		Ph.D	B	10.53	0	7.7869	26.92	1.916	12.35	6.14	5.941	15.11	6.827
			G	15.46	0.625	3.4314	16.72	1.397	6.667	5.031	2.094	10.06	4.27
			T	12.21	0.402	5.8036	22.37	1.772	9.429	5.495	4.268	13.02	5.898
	ProfEdn	Eng	B	10.17	9.891	13.069	12.18	31.64	4.97	4.262	12.05	74.39	7.355
			G	11.4	7.326	17.52	17.34	15.79	1.622	4.559	10.63	15.18	7.517
			T	10.32	9.382	14.022	13.14	24.68	4.219	4.321	11.75	33.99	7.395
		Med	B	10.41	16.52	4.5963	16.1	2.178	11.13	11.19	10.64	8.962	10.71
			G	18.6	12.42	4.8739	15.34	2.214	3.653	10.34	10.28	19.43	11.02
			T	12.55	13.99	4.6512	15.81	2.186	9.231	10.68	10.45	13.26	10.84
		Edn	B	19.4	23.77	20.871	34.79	14.46	18.33	17.02	15.55	16.98	15.15
			G	13.87	15.8	10.87	20.52	7.049	11.56	10.69	9.816	16.44	10.95
			T	16.75	18.09	15.995	25.65	12.11	14.5	11.29	12.23	16.61	13.33
2005	GenEdn	UG	B	6.78	11.9	17.014	17.55	18.82	15.19	6.017	10.69	18.51	14.34
			G	6.903	9.926	9.1998	12.79	15.85	13.05	5.561	8.592	11.18	11.67
			T	6.809	10.83	14.012	14.95	17.58	14.37	5.758	9.551	14.12	13.22
		PG	B	7.354	11.61	23.867	14.91	18.29	13.95	9.037	9.964	14.07	15.6
			G	4.001	7.055	9.9158	11.4	9.637	9.222	6.565	7.356	12.6	10.03
			T	6.337	8.251	17.028	12.94	14.76	12.06	7.747	8.469	13.32	13.02
		Ph.D	B	6.667	2.262	20.085	17.04	2.384	22	14.14	4.87	11.97	11.2

State				Orissa	Punjab	Rajasthan	TN	U P	W B	Chandigarh	Delhi	Pondicherry	India
			G	7.471	0.949	3.4826	8.329	2.279	6.061	9.412	2.771	12.12	8.016
			T	6.922	1.49	12.414	12.2	2.349	14.07	11.15	3.816	12.03	9.937
	ProfEdn	Eng	B	5.557	7.485	5.8291	8.913	20.66	12.42	23.17	14.41	16.81	9.836
			G	41.48	5.327	3.4486	8.561	9.454	9.125	19.02	17.83	16.78	9.676
			T	9.214	7	5.432	8.799	18.98	11.83	22.23	14.83	16.8	9.793
		Med	B	13.64	18.42	17.225	16.12	20.9	11.18	11.66	14.98	12.86	14.97
			G	16.14	13.08	17.085	16.35	22.53	23.88	11.26	15.46	15.19	14.26
			T	14.04	14.73	17.184	16.25	20.88	14.4	11.39	15.25	13.93	14.63
		Edn	B	16.44	19.38	13.491	23.12	19.72	19.72	19.23	9.287	28.27	17.12
			G	15.27	15.12	10.169	22.67	19.18	11.42	12.71	12.2	16.25	15.04
			T	16.01	16.07	12.002	22.81	19.55	16.72	13.89	10.75	19.93	16.21

The Table 4.1 gives the picture about the enrolment trends of Scheduled Caste students in higher education at varied levels in different states of India. The table has been diagrammatically represented for each state (Figures 4.1-4.22). For the convenience of analysis, the entire period of 14 years from 1591 is divided into 3 points of time i.e. 1991, 2001, and 2005. From the table it is evident that there is no clear trend that is emerging. While some states display steep growth in general courses there are states which register declining growth in number of Scheduled Caste students enrolled.

However one thing is conspicuous from the table when analyzed along with the population share of Scheduled Caste in the age group of 18-24 (Table 4.2 and 4.3) i.e. of higher education in all the states, that none of the states have registered enrolment of Scheduled Caste students to the level of their population and their enrolment is below such level in all the courses.

Scenario at the Level of Different States of India

To have a better picture of the enrolment trends it is more significant to have a distinct analysis of different states for per cent share of Scheduled Caste students in different disciplines at higher education level.

Andhra Pradesh—This is a state where large no. of Private higher educational institutions are established albeit it is governed by government norms. Here, except the courses at UG level (in total), MBBS, and Education, none of the courses is having participation of Scheduled Caste students as per their population which is around 16 per cent of total population in the age group. Though there has been growth in enrolment share of Scheduled Caste students since the level of 1991 in all the courses, there is declining trend visible in Engineering since 2001 when their share was 12.98 to reach 10.73 per cent in 2005. This can be due to the large number of private institutions in Andhra Pradesh to provide engineering course. (see Figure 4.1).

Table 4.2: State wise Total Population and SC Population in 2001

2001						
	Total Population			SC Population		
State	Male	Female	Total	Male	Female	Persons
Andhra Pradesh	5138987	5065755	10204742	795236	809621	1604857
Arunachal Pradesh	67021	62747	129768	467	313	780
Assam	1701538	1667085	3368623	121219	109874	231093
Bihar	6456470	5989407	12445877	864892	872573	1737465
Goa	105001	91948	196949	1882	1814	3696
Gujarat	3657582	3264726	6922308	273120	233513	506633
Haryana	1591697	1261584	2853281	304524	237632	542156
Himachal Pradesh	427940	406097	834037	103522	98389	201911
Jammu & Kashmir	705994	623688	1329682	56623	49207	105830
Karnataka	3767701	3454208	7221909	570717	530003	1100720
Kerala	2063661	2191611	4255272	211555	230252	441807
Madhya Pradesh	5179852	4687164	9867016	732710	644590	1377300
Maharashtra	6973542	5830156	12803698	683922	597106	1281028
Manipur	159333	161852	321185	4023	4245	8268
Meghalaya	143465	148900	292365	746	626	1372
Mizoram	68482	65266	133748	31	7	38
Nagaland	169003	152377	321380	0	0	0
Orissa	2337686	2291237	4628923	370760	354587	725347
Punjab	1838810	1547872	3386682	518611	430273	948884
Rajasthan	3649127	3254416	6903543	621676	536978	1158654
Sikkim	43304	37730	81034	2012	2136	4148
Tamil Nadu	4209094	4243716	8452810	791688	814370	1606058
Tripura	201577	204254	405831	37300	36868	74168
Uttar Pradesh	11155731	9634888	20790619	2202824	1903584	4106408
West Bengal	5214322	4980892	10195214	1198402	1168882	2367284
Andaman & Nicobar Islands	30075	24681	54756	0	0	0
Chandigarh	85528	59122	144650	13532	10671	24203
Dadra & Nagar Haveli	22291	13936	36227	357	319	676
Daman & Diu	23973	9935	33908	421	337	758
Delhi	1167022	850732	2017754	197276	153469	350745
Lakshadweep	4062	4076	8138	0	0	0
Pondicherry	69328	71034	140362	11377	11743	23120
India	68429199	62353092	130782291	10691425	9843982	20535407

Table 4.3: Percent Share of SC Population (estimated) in 2005

State	2005		
	Boys	Girls	Total
Andhra Pradesh	15.47	15.93	15.70
Arunachal Pradesh	0.00	0.00	0.00
Assam	7.10	6.57	6.84
Bihar	13.36	14.46	13.88
Goa	2.06	2.35	2.20
Gujarat	7.49	7.17	7.34
Haryana	19.14	18.78	18.98
Himachal Pradesh	23.80	23.92	23.86
Jammu & Kashmir	7.92	7.74	7.84
Karnataka	15.03	15.37	15.19
Kerala	10.07	10.32	10.20
Madhya Pradesh	14.18	13.73	13.97
Maharashtra	9.80	10.24	10.00
Manipur	2.67	2.63	2.65
Meghalaya	0.73	0.71	0.72
Mizoram	0.00	0.00	0.00
Nagaland	0.00	0.00	0.00
Orissa	15.87	15.48	15.68
Punjab	28.31	20.22	24.58
Rajasthan	17.06	16.41	16.76
Sikkim	5.00	5.71	5.33
Tamil Nadu	18.30	18.82	18.56
Tripura	18.42	18.23	18.32
Uttar Pradesh	19.82	19.64	19.74
West Bengal	22.63	23.00	22.81
Andaman & Nicobar Islands	0.00	0.00	0.00
Chandigarh	16.46	18.52	17.29
Dadra & Nagar Haveli	0.00	0.00	0.00
Daman & Diu	0.00	0.00	0.00
Delhi	17.03	18.24	17.54
Lakshadweep	0.00	0.00	0.00
Pondicherry	17.19	16.67	16.92
India	15.55	15.49	15.52

Source: Selected Educational Statistics.

Assam—In Assam the population figures for Scheduled Castes are not available and therefore its analysis is comparably weak. There has been a decline on enrolment share of higher education of Scheduled Caste students except the course of engineering which has increased for 6.44 in 1991 to 13.37 per cent in 2005. In the

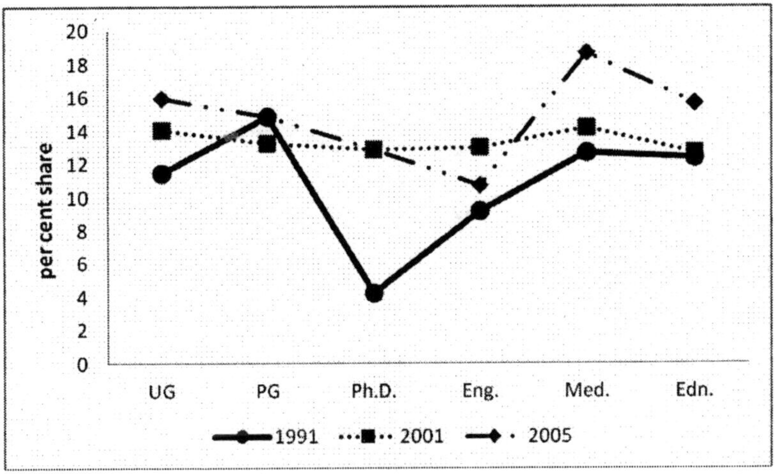

Figure 4.1: Percent Share of SCs in Higher Education in Andhra Pradesh

course of engineering and medicine there is significant grown for 5.64 in 1991 to 13.87 in 2005 for engineering and from 6.44 in medical to 7.65 per cent in 2005. (see Figure 4.2).

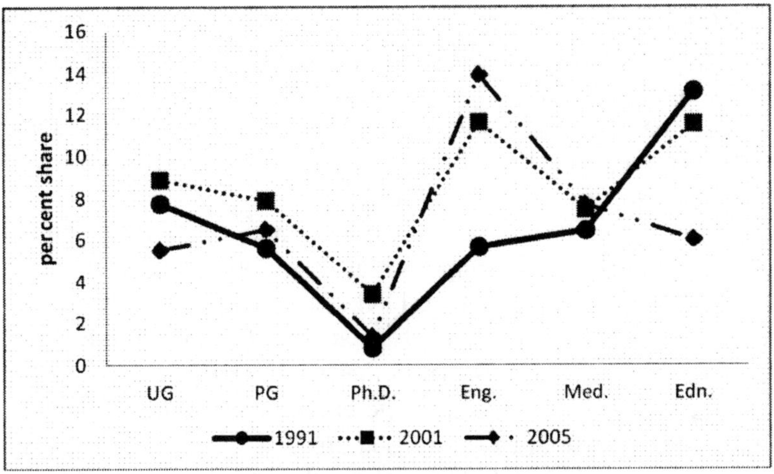

Figure 4.2: Percent Share of SCs in Higher Education in Assam

Bihar—In Bihar (including Jharkhand) data was available only for 2001 and 2005. From the available data of enrolment percent

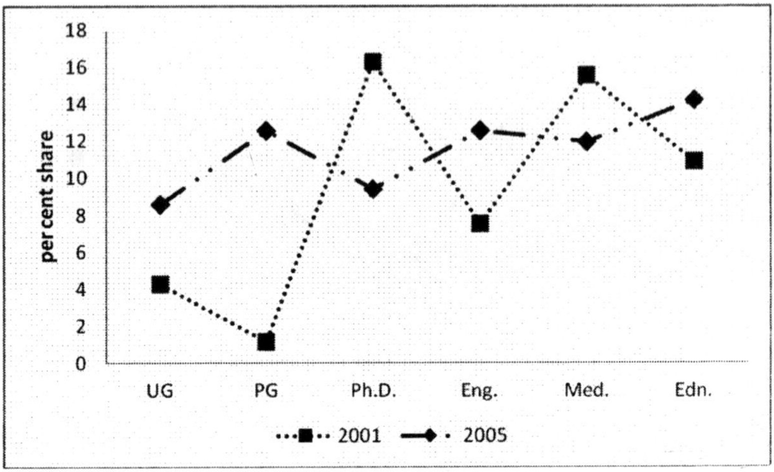

Figure 4.3: Percent Share of SCs in Higher Education in Bihar

share of Scheduled Caste students in higher education it comes out that only in education discipline their participation percent matches with their population figures i.e. 14 per cent from 11 per cent in 2001. It is important to note down that the state's data as available in SES shows growth of 12 times in the total courses offered at PG level for 2001 level of 1.13 per cent which seems to be an error in estimate. Apart from this, engineering and total UG courses has registered a growth of 5 and 4 per cent respectively whereas there is decline of similar percentage in Ph.D and Medical courses respectively (see Figure 4.3).

Goa—The state of Goa is having merely 2.22 percent of population in the age-group for higher education as estimated for 2005. In respect to this, Goa is having equal number of Scheduled Caste students in Medical and Education field which has declined in case of medical course from the level of 5.17 in 1991. Also, decline in share is noticed in the engineering courses apart for marginal increase in UG and PG courses.

Gujarat—The state has registered a marginal growth on all the professional courses while a similar decline is observed from the table for UG, PG and Ph.D courses from 2001 level. (see Figure 4.5)

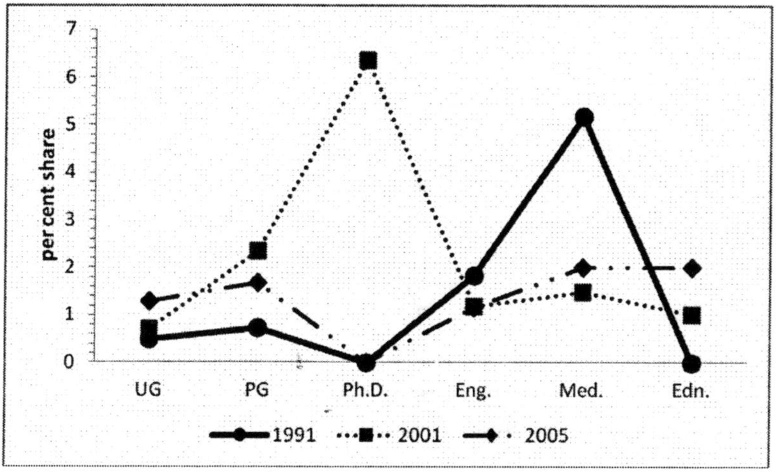

Figure 4.4: Percent Share of SCs in Higher Education in Goa

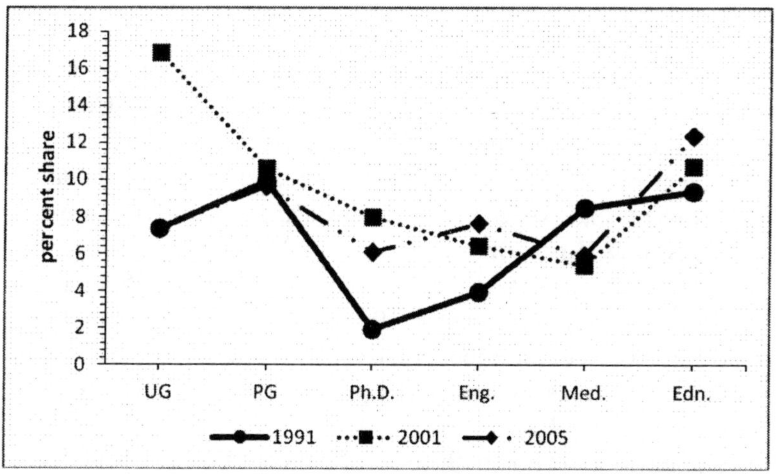

Figure 4.5: Percent Share of SCs in Higher Education in Gujarat

Haryana—The state of Haryana is far behind in terms of enrolment of Scheduled Caste students in higher education in proportion to their population which is around 19 per cent for 2005. There is decline of 3, 4 and 1 per cent for PG courses, Ph.D. and Education in respective term to reach 10.77, 8.21 and 14.31 per cent in 2005. Also there is decline of almost 11 per cent for the engineering courses' enrolment for Scheduled Caste students (Fig. 4.6).

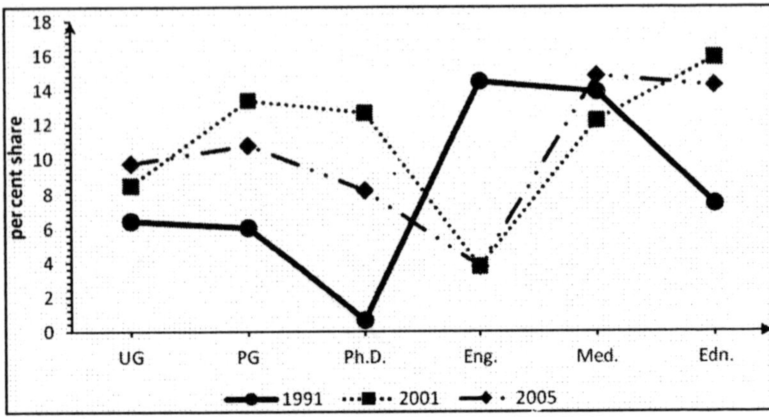

Figure 4.6: Percent Share of SCs in Higher Education in Haryana

Himachal Pradesh—The state is having 24 per cent of Scheduled Caste students in the category of higher education while the respective enrolment is not beyond 13. Also, the table and graph clearly shows the decline on participation of Scheduled Caste students in terms of enrolment in all courses except PG Courses. Though there is marginal increase of 2 per cent in Medical courses but such growth is unable to out do the per cent share of Scheduled Caste students that existed in 1991 in medical course. (see Figure 4.7)

Jammu & Kashmir—The data for 2001 are not available for the state and if we analyse the position of enrolment of Scheduled Caste students between level of 1991 and 2005, there is magional growth in UG, PG, and Education courses while there is decline in engneering courses to reach 2.17 per cent in 2005 from 6.17 in 1991. (see Figure 4.8)

Karnataka—Though the overall per cent share of Scheduled Caste students has increased in various courses in the period of study except PG, PhD and Education, the total per cent share of Scheduled Caste students in the state is less than their actual population percentage. (see Figure 4.9)

Kerala—The state has more then 10 per cent of Scheduled Caste pop in the higher education Age-group. The state's educational advancement at lower level is reflected in higher education participation of Scheduled Castes. The per cent share

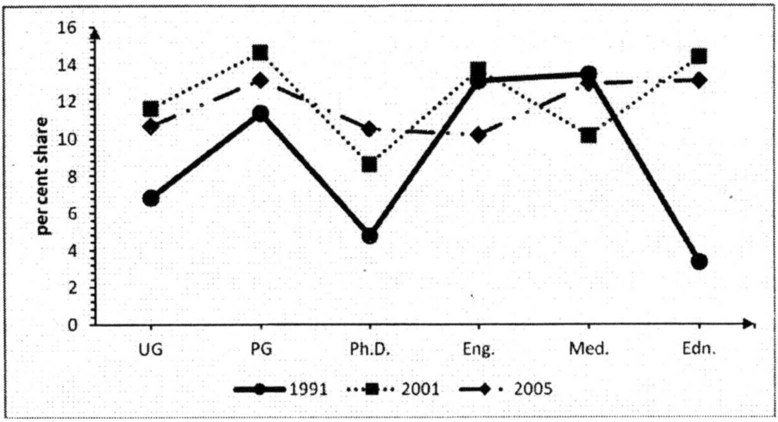

Figure 4.7: Percent Share of SCs in Higher Education in Himachal Pradesh

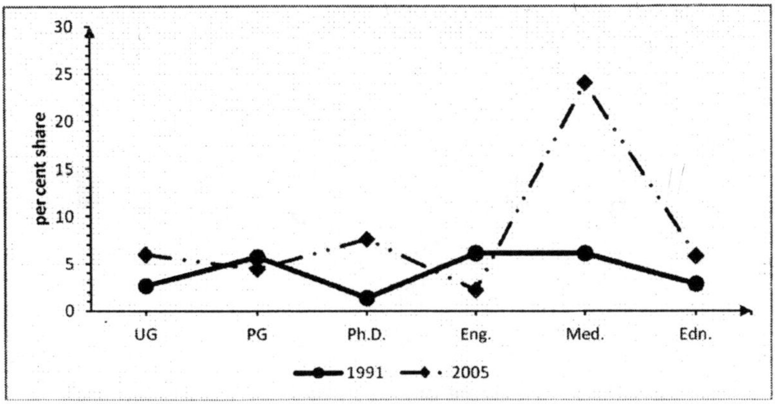

Figure 4.8: Percent Share of SCs in Higher Education in Jammu & Kashmir

of Scheduled Castes has increased or all the courses except Ph.D course. (see Figure 4.10)

Madhya Pradesh—The share of M.P. (including Chhatisgarh) has shown a manifold increase in per cent share of Scheduled Castes in total higher education in India since 1991 level. It appears that data have been inflated or erroneously calculated to estimate enrolment of Scheduled Caste students. (see Figure 4.11)

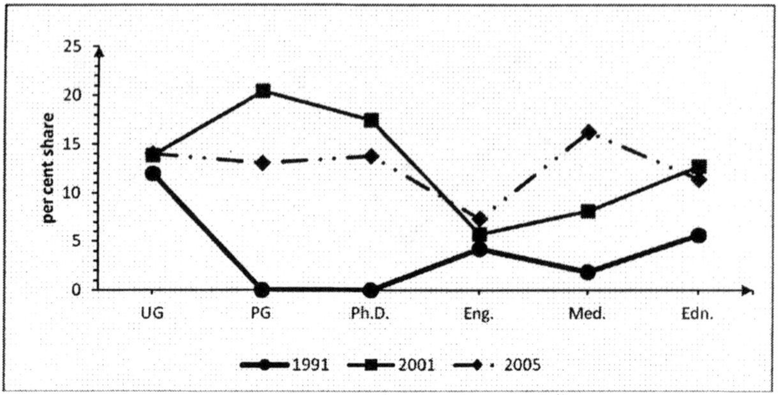

Figure 4.9: Percent Share of SCs in Higher Education in Karnataka

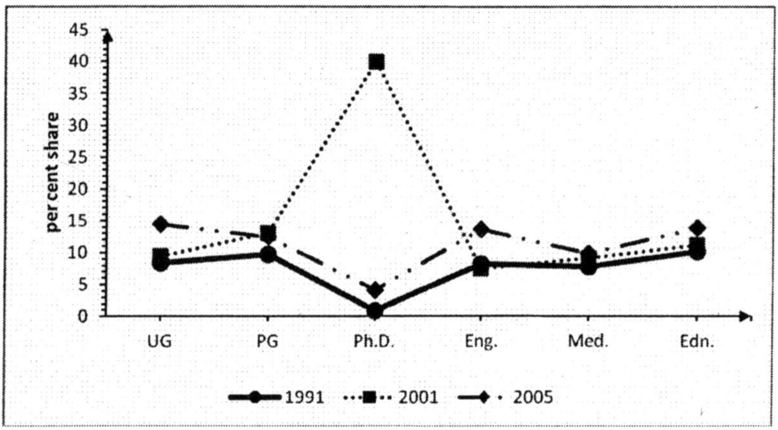

Figure 4.10: Percent Share of SCs in Higher Education in Kerala

Maharashtra—There has been overall decline in per cent share of Scheduled Castes in different courses except Ph.D and Medical course which have registered a marginal increase in enrolment of Scheduled Caste students. (see Figure 4.12)

Orissa—Except the UG courses, medical and education, there is negative trend since 1991. The overall per cent share of Scheduled Caste students' higher education in Orissa of around 7 per cent which is 8 per cent less than their relevant population.

Punjab—On the basis of estimated population figures for higher education, it can be said that maximum number of Scheduled Caste

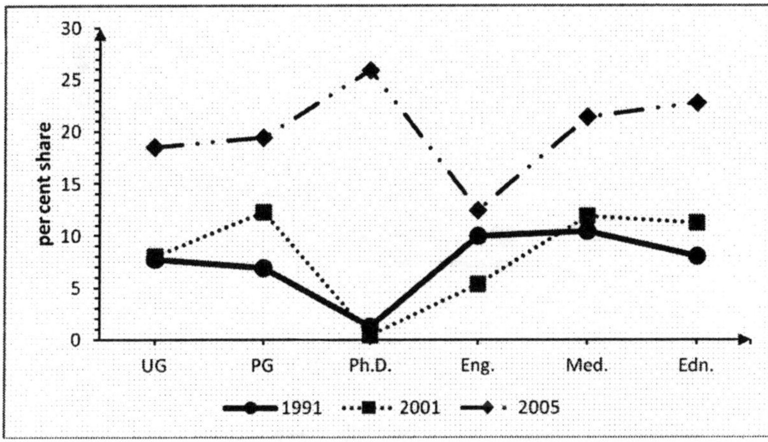

Figure 4.11: Percent Share of SCs in Higher Education in Madhya Pradesh

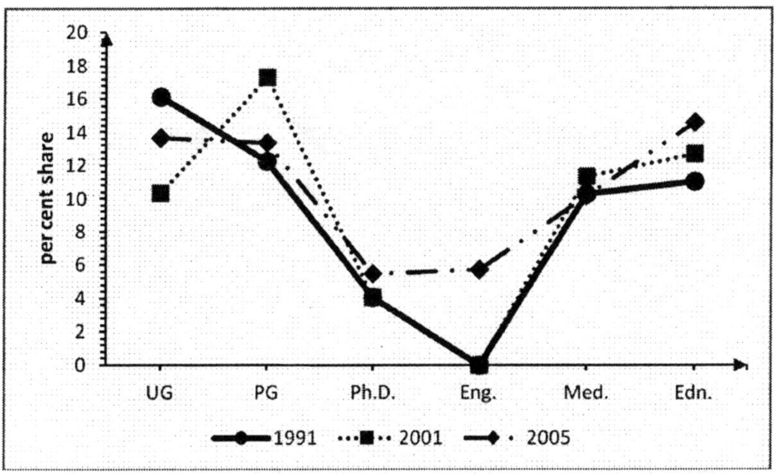

Figure 4.12: Percent Share of SCs in Higher Education in Maharashtra

students hails from Punjab. There is around 25 per cent of Scheduled Caste population, while their per cent share has increased marginally to reach level of 10.83, 8.25, 14.73 and 16.07 in BG, PG, MBBS, and Educate respectively on 2005. (see Figure 4.14)

Rajasthan—In Rajasthan the enrolment of Scheduled Castes has increased in general courses of UG, PG, and Ph.D. while there

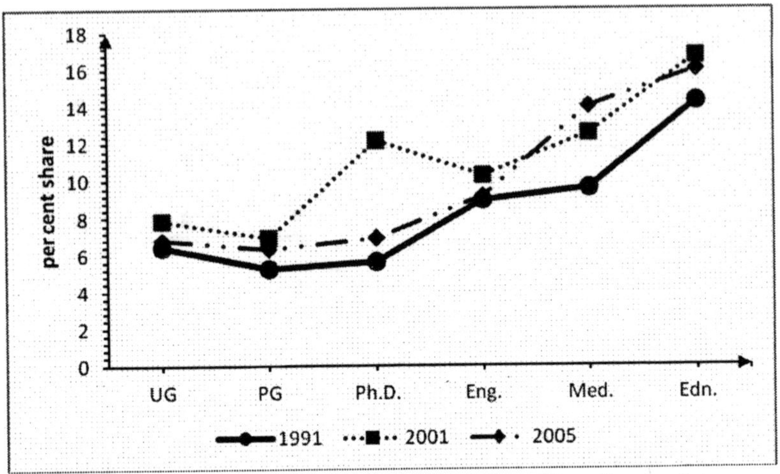

Figure 4.13: Percent Share of SCs in Higher Education in Orissa

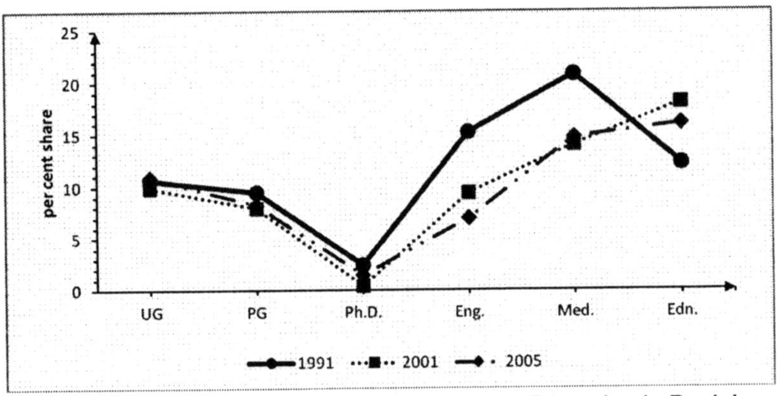

Figure 4.14: Percent Share of SCs in Higher Education in Punjab

is decline of same or professional courses e.g. in engineering from 14.02 per cent enrolment it has come to 5.43 per cent in 2005. (see Figure 4.15)

Tamil Nadu—This state shows decline in enrolment of Scheduled Caste student in entire higher education except Medical course where increase of 1 per cent is registered. This might be the result of mushrooming of private institutions in the state. (see Figure 4.16)

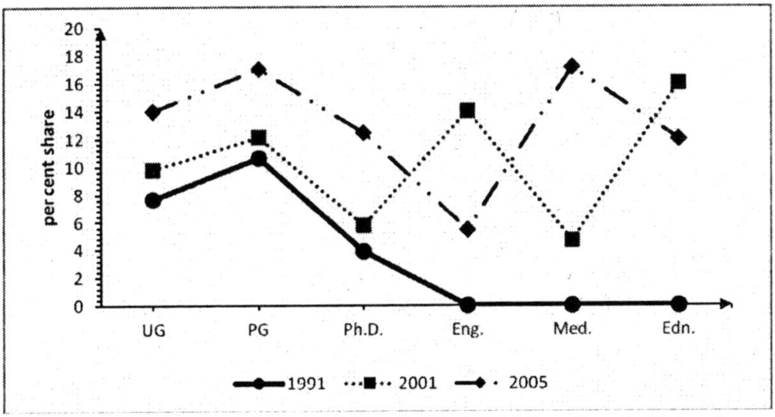

Figure 4.15: Percent Share of SCs in Higher Education in Rajasthan

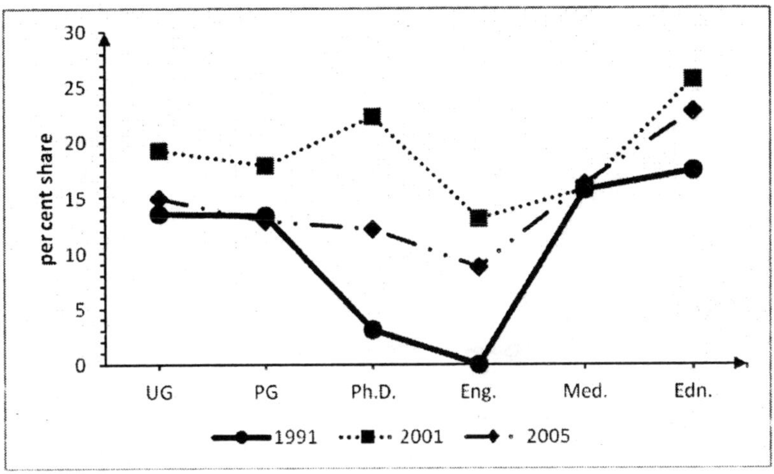

Figure 4.16: Percent Share of SCs in Higher Education in Tamil Nadu

U.P. – In the state of U.P. (including Uttarakhand), apart from an overall marginal increase in the enrolment of Scheduled Castes in higher education, there is decline of Scheduled Caste students on engineering courses in 2005 for 24.68 in 2001 to 18.98 in 2005. (see Figure 4.17)

W.B. – In West Bengal there resides around 23 per cent of Scheduled Castes in for age group of 18-24 years, however despite growth from 1991 and 2001 level the outcome low participate of Scheduled Castes. (see Figure 4.18)

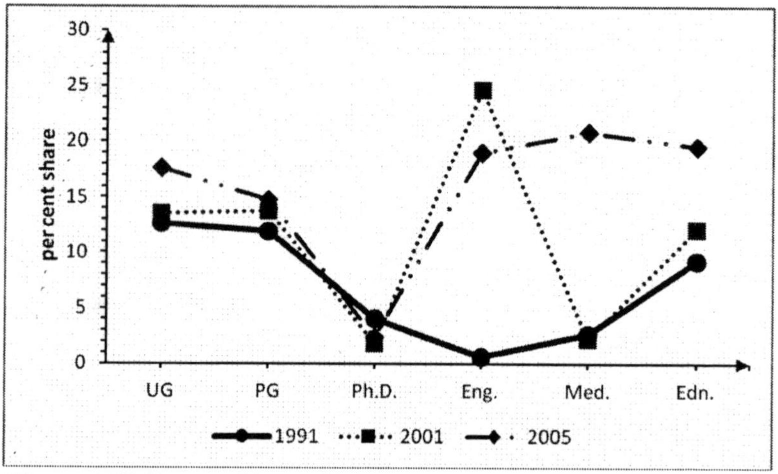

Figure 4.17: Percent Share of SCs in Higher Education in Uttar Pradesh

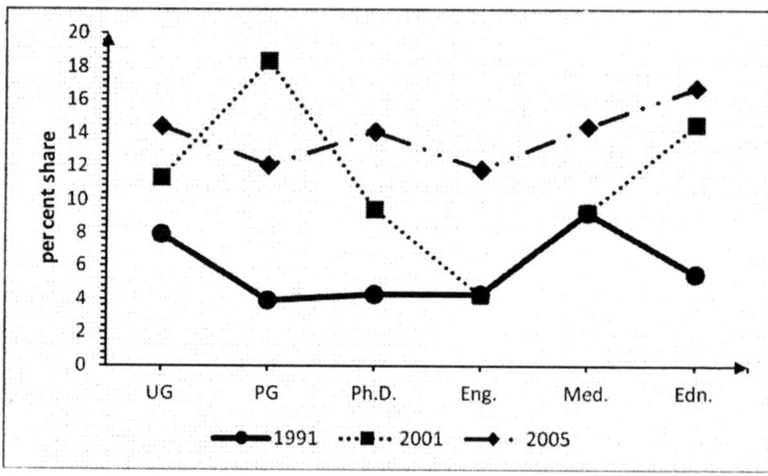

Figure 4.18: Percent Share of SCs in Higher Education in West Bengal

Chandigarh (Union Territory) – There is overall growth of Scheduled Caste students after a look towards graph mentioning the same however there is an exception of UG courses where the share has declined to 5.75 per cent in 2005 from 2.88 in 1991. (see Figure 4.19)

Delhi (National Capital Territory) – The state of Delhi is having fairly good amount (18 per cent) of Scheduled Castes. In the state, there is trend of decline in Ph.D, Engineering and Education courses with a reduction of 1, 3, and 2 per cent for Ph.D, Engineering, and Education courses. And final per cent share is 3.81, 14.83 and 10.75 in 2005. (see Figure 4.20)

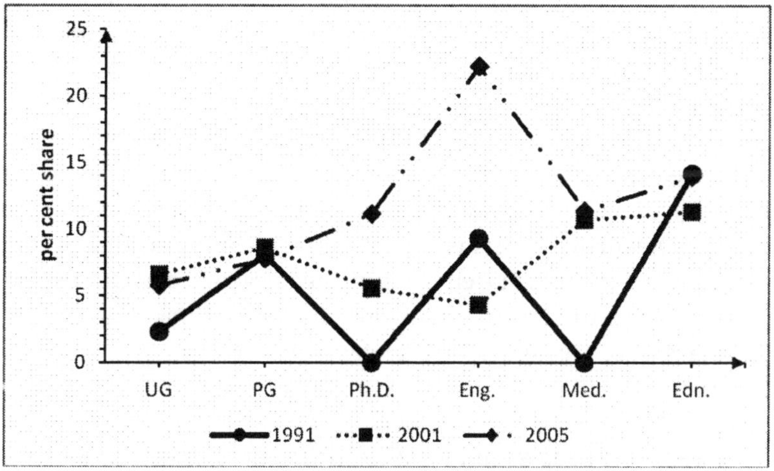

Figure 4.19: Percent Share of SCs in Higher Education in Chandigarh (U.T)

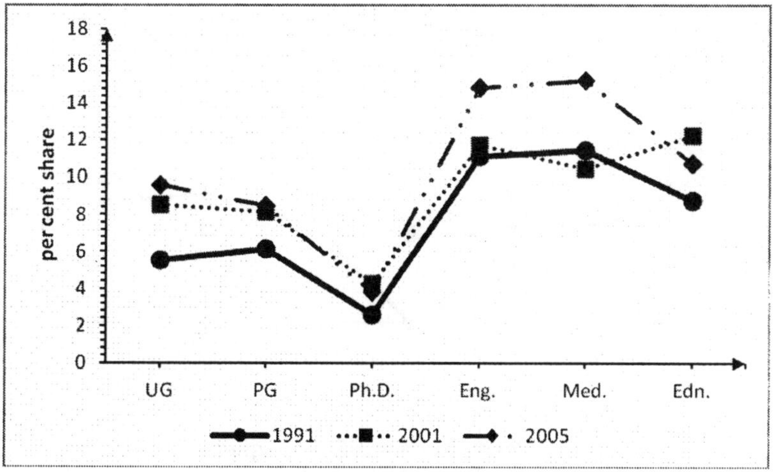

Figure 4.20: Percent Share of SCs in Higher Education in Delhi (N.C.T)

Pondicherry (Union Territory) – The state's figure shows steep decline in course of Engineering from 33.99 to 16.8 per cent share. (see Figure 4.21)

Overall picture for India which emerges for the table is that there is growth in enrolment percentage of Scheduled Caste student in higher education as a result of affirmative action as well as other factors. But such growth of nominal in all the courses except medical and education courses where the growth of more prominent against general education course. And most importantly, their enrolment is still less than their respective population.

The table makes it clear that there is certain growth in the enrolment per cent of SC students in various courses at higher education level in 2005 when compared with the level existent in 1991. The growth seems to be more prominent among the professional courses like engineering, medical and education. This growth is due to effective intervention by government in form of scholarships, freeships, hostel facilities, etc. and to provide reservations. (Prakash: 2008). Also, the growth can be attributed to new initiative by UGC in 2005 to establish special cells in the universities to keep a vigil for the fulfillment of the reserved seats by the students of the same category (Kale, 2008). Further in special respect, A.P. has registered a growth in enrolment of SCs, however

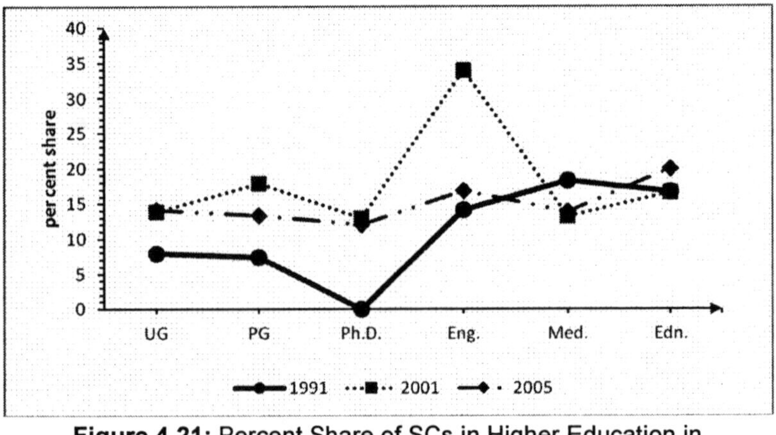

Figure 4.21: Percent Share of SCs in Higher Education in Pondicherry (U.T)

this reflection of grabbing the opportunity by the Christians of the state who are developed and are staying in the urban districts (Chalam, 1988). In critical terms, such a growth could have been a surmised one as the increased enrolment numbers may indicate more number of repeaters from the SC category in the professional courses (Sinha, 2009) as the educational performance of SC students has recorded to be bad (RLSCST 26th (1978-79). There are states as Assam, Delhi (NCT), Kerala, Chandigarh (U.T.) where the performance of SC students have increased as an impact of industrialization as it has been for A.P. in previous years (Chatterjee, 2001). In states like U.P., T.N., Maharashtra, Pondicherry and Goa, decline in Professional course of engineering or medical is noticed which may be a result of increase in private institutions. There seems to be erroneous data, an obvious limitation of using secondary data (Best and Kahn: 2006), in case of figures provided by Bihar, M.P. and Haryana where a sudden sleep inflation in terms of enrolment is noticed. Further, it has to be clearly understood that though the growth is registered in enrolment figures for higher education, such growth doesn't satisfy the population percent of SC students (Table-Enrolment). Also, the NSSO 61st round mentions that a marginal percent of SCs in 17-30 age group is in higher education where 2.1 per cent is from rural and 6.7 per cent for urban background (Sundaram, 2007).

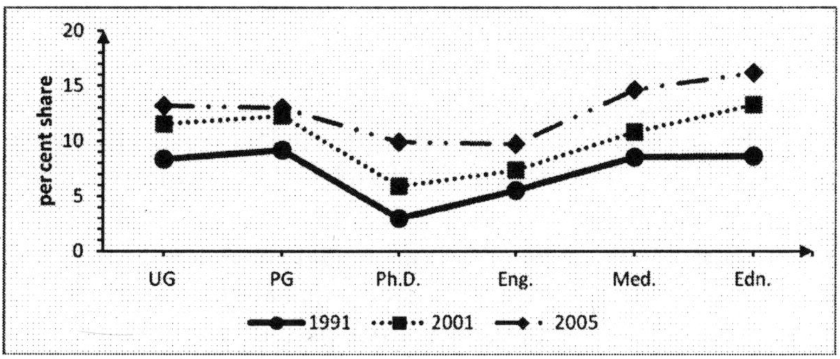

Figure 4.22: Percent Share of SCs in Higher Education in India

4.2 Growth Rate among SC and General Category Students

The tables (4.4.1 and 4.4.2) are about the compared annual growth rate in terms of enrolment of Scheduled Caste students in comparison with unreserved students in different courses at various levels of higher education in all Indian states. In order to note down the impact of growth of private colleges to impart higher education, the study is divided into two periods, one from 1991 and 1991, and second period between 1997 and 2005 as the number of private colleges (unaided) has increased to the level of 51.37 per cent on 2005-06 (Anandkrishnan, 2006). The entire study on comparison can be better understood if looked distinctly for different states.

Andhra Pradesh—In the state of A.P. there is increase in the annual growth rate for Scheduled Caste students enrolled in various courses of higher education in the second period (1997 and 2005) when compared with first (1991 and 1997). During the same time periods there is increase in enrolment of unreserved or general students in all the courses. When compared the annual growth rate of Scheduled Castes with General students, rise in same is more prominent among the former than the latter in all the courses except in Engineering, and PG where the annual growth rate of general students is more in the second period. The compound average growth rate for first period (1991 and 1997) was -0.15and 2.69 for general and Scheduled Caste students in respective terns for PG course which increased to 13.87 and 11.93 respectively for 2nd period. And for engineering course the growth rate was 4.12 and 11.79 for general and Scheduled Caste students respectively for the first period which rose to 35.41 and 31.43 in respective terms for the second period.

Assam—In the state of Assam, annual enrolment growth rate of Scheduled Caste students has declined in all the courses for the second period in comparison to first period, while there is an increase in growth rate of general category for Ph.D and Medical course for the said period. The decline in growth rate for Scheduled Caste students is high and it has become negative for all the courses

Table 4.4.1: Growth Rate of SC Students in Higher Education

		State	*A P*	*Assam*	*Bihar*	*Goa*	*Gujarat*	*Haryana*	*H P*	*J & K*	*Karnataka*	*Kerala*	*M P*	*Maharashtra*
Gen	UG	1991	24260	8010	0	53	20770	5458	580	598	21342	7054	14917	69669
		1997	29227	14706	16606	75	22884	7067	5619	1199	36411	12344	23854	78936
		Growth	3.15	10.66	*	5.96	1.63	4.40	46.01	12.29	9.31	9.77	8.14	2.10
		2005	95669	10542	52988	187	30582	16799	8438	5785	41090	22533	56402	91888
		Cagr	15.98	-4.08	15.61	12.10	3.69	11.43	5.21	21.74	1.52	7.81	11.36	1.92
	PG	1991	2440	257	0	6	2590	307	159	123	0	678	2501	8533
		1997	2861	786	873	7	3755	1011	357	116	1419	1876	3766	12051
		Growth	2.69	20.48	*	2.60	6.39	21.97	14.43	-0.97	*	18.49	7.06	5.92
		2005	7049	504	5586	18	8135	1895	424	371	3106	2827	10950	9207
		cagr	11.93	-5.40	26.11	12.53	10.15	8.17	2.17	15.64	10.29	5.26	14.27	-3.31
	Ph.D	1991	72	2	N.A.	0	25	9	37	6	N.A.	10	29	194
		1997	72	11	67	0	65	86	35	0	307	135	40	144
		Growth	0	32.86	*	*	17.26	45.67	-0.92	-100.00	*	54.31	5.51	-4.85
		2005	787	6	202	0	78	158	208	70	428	14	677	113
		Cagr	34.84	-7.30	14.79	*	2.31	7.90	24.95	*	4.24	-24.67	42.42	-2.98
Prof	Eng	1991	2039	157	N.A.	13	550	369	27	32	2100	790	261	2329
		1997	3980	432	207	10	1243	685	98	44	3622	669	1472	3725
		Growth	11.79	18.38	*	-4.28	14.56	10.86	23.97	5.45	9.51	-2.73	33.42	8.14
		2005	35433	384	2093	31	2440	1814	436	223	12477	12587	12012	9981
		Cagr	31.43	-1.46	33.54	15.19	8.80	12.95	20.51	22.49	16.72	44.32	30.01	13.11

* Calculation is not possible due to insufficient data.

		State	A P	Assam	Bihar	Goa	Gujarat	Haryana	H P	J & K	Karnataka	Kerala	M P	Maharashtra
	Med	1991	979	131	N.A.	14	550	160	46	82	138	262	476	1354
		1997	1086	176	1490	15	788	376	108	98	201	305	531	2791
		Growth	1.74	5.04	*	1.16	6.18	15.30	15.29	3.02	6.47	2.57	1.84	12.81
		2005	4295	230	1489	19	727	698	247	219	11100	906	2960	5821
		Cagr	18.75	3.40	-0.01	3.00	-1.00	8.04	10.89	10.57	65.11	14.58	23.96	9.62
	Edn	1991	962	158	N.A.	0	450	260	6	29	402	311	444	2069
		1997	1020	314	197	0	541	437	69	39	1050	546	499	4338
		Growth	0.98	12.13	*	*	3.12	9.04	50.24	5.06	17.35	9.83	1.97	13.13
		2005	5674	153	1387	4	1550	550	448	45	772	478	2304	2277
		Cagr	23.93	-8.59	27.63	*	14.06	2.92	26.34	1.80	-3.77	-1.65	21.07	-7.74

Source: Selected Educational Statistics.

Table 4.4.1 (Contd.)

		State	Orissa	Punjab	Rajasthan	TN	Tripura	UP	WB	Chandigarh	Delhi	Pondicherry	India
Gen	UG	1991	4335	NA	5629	26332	987	44654	NA	216	6325	298	294903
		1997	9630	NA	16202	36456	1790	70682	NA	850	4877	758	432001
		Growth	14.228	8	19.27	5.5717	10.43	7.9547	1.11	25.65	-4.24	16.836	6.5698
		2005	12114	NA	39270	62781	3569	229855	NA	1395	11224	1610	894039
		Cagr	2.91	2.8	11.7	7.0305	9.009	15.883	15.4	6.3884	10.98	9.8739	9.5176
	PG	1991	509	533	1157	2759	46	10901	665	154	607	21	34969

		State	Orissa	Punjab	Rajasthan	TN	Tripura	UP	WB	Chandigarh	Delhi	Pondicherry	India
		1997	627	753	2295	2358	153	19778	750	107	329	313	56431
		Growth	3.5361	5.9	12.09	-2.584	22.18	10.438	2.02	-5.8883	-9.704	56.875	8.3027
		2005	909	NA	4540	8493	260	36982	8974	303	655	220	113109
		cagr	4.7519	10	8.902	17.372	6.853	8.1374	36.4	13.896	8.988	-4.311	9.0806
	Ph.D	1991	19	19	6	5	0	324	55	0	126	0	938
		1997	29	8	13	122	0	166	7	2	129	9	1463
		Growth	7.3019	-13	13.75	70.307	0	-10.55	-29.1	*	0.393	*	7.6896
		2005	38	8	54	427	1	49	56	30	159	57	3629
		Cagr	3.4364	0	19.48	16.952	*	-14.15	29.7	40.285	2.648	25.952	12.026
Prof	Eng	1991	229	342	0	2314	70	89	332	196	436	83	12758
		1997	365	936	0	4308	123	89	2005	61	413	218	24705
		Growth	8.0794	18	-	10.914	9.85	0	34.9	-17.679	-0.899	17.462	11.644
		2005	4179	0	3040	28971	148	21693	6464	986	2798	1314	163376
		Cagr	35.627	19	-	26.9	2.34	98.777	15.8	41.602	27.02	25.175	26.634
	Med	1991	175	476	N.A.	1184	0	181	348	0	468	101	7137
		1997	294	577	0	1470	0	181	348	0	117	241	11205
		Growth	9.0314	3.3	-	3.6719	0	0	0	*	-20.63	15.598	7.8076
		2005	1000	0	1405	6360	47	3079	570	135	1356	382	44721
		Cagr	16.535	13	-	20.093	*	42.509	6.36	*	35.83	5.9268	18.888

* Calculation not possible due to insufficient data.

		State	Orissa	Punjab	Rajasthan	TN	Tripura	UP	WB	Chandigarh	Delhi	Pondicherry	India
	Edn	1991	195	399	N.A.	501	28	1552	512	68	71	20	8437
		1997	254	641	1180	580	85	1610	481	59	75	83	14127
		Growth	4.5041	8.2	-	2.4704	20.33	0.6134	-1.04	-2.3384	0.918	26.768	8.9708
		2005	317	774	1427	2241	95	9375	1439	100	492	428	32366
		Cagr	2.8083	2.4	2.404	18.407	1.4	24.636	14.7	6.8178	26.51	22.757	10.919

Source: Selected Educational Statistics.

Table 4.4.2: Growth Rate of General Students in Higher Education

	States	A.P	Assam	Bihar	Goa	Gujarat	Haryana	H.P.	J&K	Karnata	Kerala	M.P.	Mahara	Orissa
UG	1991	184413	87316	454922	11099	239880	79900	7717	22290	*	77692	168017	549540	59955
	1997	257202	125042	557098	12317	268713	98643	48128	40065	299831	126505	165927	584186	117714
	CAGR	5.70	6.17	3.43	1.75	1.91	3.57	35.67	10.27	*	8.46	-0.21	1.02	11.90
	2005	477589	159479	554577	14144	349842	155169	66597	83090	239863	131847	218099	536591	157511
	CAGR	8.04	3.09	-0.06	1.74	3.35	5.83	4.14	9.55	-2.75	0.52	3.48	-1.06	3.71
PG	1991	13630	4031	27700	833	21435	4788	1167	2018	13569	6326	32345	60097	8942
	1997	13508	8351	29236	767	26645	8368	2758	3149	8569	13924	26248	55658	9787
	CAGR	-0.15	12.91	0.90	-1.37	3.69	9.75	15.41	7.70	-7.37	14.05	-3.42	-1.27	1.52
	2005	38177	6167	36528	1024	67017	15693	2551	7604	19965	19695	36881	57087	12919
	CAGR	13.87	-3.72	2.82	3.68	12.22	8.18	-0.97	11.65	11.15	4.43	4.34	0.32	3.53

	States	A.P	Assam	Bihar	Goa	Gujarat	Haryana	H.P.	J&K	Karnata	Kerala	M.P.	Mahara	Orissa
Ph.D	1991	1613	230	731	0	1260	1435	727	428	520	1041	2263	4576	300
	1997	1618	273	634	144	865	1015	657	286	1559	1963	8582	3555	336
	CAGR	0.052	2.90	-2.34	*	-6.08	-5.61	-1.67	-6.50	20.08	11.15	24.88	-4.12	1.91
	2005	5189	426	1800	68	1125	1767	1715	756	2614	324	1572	1938	490
	CAGR	15.68	5.72	13.93	-8.95	3.34	7.18	12.74	12.92	6.67	-20.16	-19.12	-7.30	4.83
Eng	1991	19910	2413	6263	697	13180	2176	165	492	46600	8713	2284	51292	2033
	1997	25374	2613	6082	885	18699	3369	595	751	68842	12609	11699	79236	4474
	CAGR	4.12	1.34	-0.49	4.06	6.00	7.56	23.83	7.30	6.72	6.35	31.29	7.52	14.05
	2005	286773	2026	13160	2584	25333	46610	3690	9734	154037	76081	62884	161481	37233
	CAGR	35.41	-3.13	10.13	14.33	3.87	38.87	25.62	37.75	10.59	25.19	23.40	9.31	30.33
Med	1991	6402	1669	NA	257	5650	990	275	1264	7121	3046	3753	11526	1476
	1997	6315	1863	13052	701	10797	2019	653	1461	4782	4042	3853	25711	2279
	CAGR	-0.23	1.85	NA	18.20	11.40	12.61	15.50	2.44	-6.42	4.83	0.44	14.31	7.51
	2005	17460	2318	10298	884	10742	4008	1570	414	52927	7910	7472	46426	5445
	CAGR	13.56	2.77	-2.92	2.94	-0.06	8.95	11.59	-14.58	35.05	8.75	8.63	7.67	11.50
Edn	1991	6453	961	NA	113	3900	3244	173	986	6691	2763	4935	16211	1012
	1997	6495	2062	2095	212	3368	3228	365	1007	2532	3640	5076	27234	1506
	CAGR	0.11	13.57	*	11.06	-2.41	-0.08	13.25	0.35	-14.95	4.70	0.47	9.03	6.85

* Calculation not possible due to insufficient data for previous year (1991).)

	States	A.P	Assam	Bihar	Goa	Gujarat	Haryana	H.P.	J&K	Karnata	Kerala	M.P.	Mahara	Orissa
	2005	29497	2067	8018	185	9678	3293	2746	658	5789	2903	6171	12158	1445
	CAGR	20.82	0.03	18.27	-1.69	14.10	0.25	28.69	-5.18	10.89	-2.79	2.47	-9.59	-0.52

Source: Selected Educational Statistics.

Table 4.4.2 (Contd. ...)

	States	Punjab	Rajasthan	Tamil	Tripura	U.P.	W.B.	Chandigarh	Delhi	Pondicherry	India
UG	1991	79247	64053	167358	8873	308728	269087	9183	108012	3468	3134723
	1997	133974	128522	238774	11161	685605	342676	18353	234799	4821	4539155
	CAGR	9.15	12.31	6.10	3.90	14.22	4.11	12.23	13.82	5.64	6.36
	2005	153229	208265	355891	13963	—	454284	22620	104591	9789	5557699
	CAGR	1.69	6.22	5.12	2.84	5.74	3.59	2.65	-9.61	9.26	2.56
PG	1991	5079	8563	17814	529	79760	16341	1752	9094	265	337523
	1997	9515	10247	21313	761	121373	19974	2010	11943	1106	406995
	CAGR	11.03	3.04	3.03	6.25	7.25	3.40	2.32	4.65	26.89	3.17
	2005	17958	19018	56859	794	211916	64256	3496	6783	1432	717819
	CAGR	8.26	8.04	13.05	0.53	7.21	15.73	7.16	-6.83	3.28	7.35
Ph.D	1991	763	146	156	0	7729	1225	84	4732	0	30058
	1997	374	135	1517	3	7907	1445	165	4502	266	38009
	CAGR	-11.20	-1.30	46.10	*	0.38	2.79	11.91	-0.83	*	3.99

* Calculation not possible due to insufficient data.

	States	Punjab	Rajasthan	Tamil	Tripura	U.P.	W.B.	Chandigarh	Delhi	Pondicherry	India
	2005	529	322	3043	10	1964	335	234	3890	417	31370
	CAGR	4.43	11.48	9.09	16.24	-15.98	-16.70	4.46	-1.81	5.78	-2.37
Eng	1991	1903	4551	24911	326	14076	7302	1879	3411	507	215084
	1997	6485	3947	34511	257	17622	7119	374	4098	1151	310939
	CAGR	22.67	-2.35	5.58	-3.89	3.82	-0.42	-23.59	3.11	14.64	6.34
	2005	49982	50783	299258	469	88337	48153.5	3403	14541	6507	1446008
	CAGR	29.08	37.62	31.00	7.81	22.32	26.99	31.79	17.15	24.18	21.18
Med	1991	1807	NA	6295	0	6688	3407	0	3580	450	73927
	1997	3737	4017	9846	0	6688	3407	40	4941	657	111050
	CAGR	12.87	-	7.74	*	0.00	0.00	*	5.52	6.51	7.02
	2005	9159	5749	32436	96	11621	3364	1021	7469	2360	241622
	CAGR	11.86	4.58	16.07	*	7.15	-0.16	49.92	5.30	17.33	10.21
Edn	1991	2867	-	2373	111	15232	8681	394	730	100	86582
	1997	2927	5474	2501	19	16119	6864	329	273	394	94303
	CAGR	0.35	-	0.88	-25.49	0.95	-3.84	-2.96	-15.12	25.68	1.43
	2005	4042	9542	7486	252	38148	6900	599	3871	1719	157928
	CAGR	4.12	7.19	14.69	38.14	11.37	0.07	7.78	39.30	20.22	6.66

* Calculation not possible due to insufficient data.

Source: Selected Educational Statistics.

except Medical where it has declined 2 per cent to reach 3.40 in second period. This implies that the enrolment of Scheduled Caste students in all the courses (except Medical) has reduced in absolute terms for 2005 from 1997. The trend of decline in annual growth rate is also seen for General category students however growth in enrolment is taking place in all courses except PG and engineering where enrolment figures have declined from the level of 1997.

Goa—for this state, figure of annual growth rate is unavailable for Ph.D and Education courses for Scheduled Caste students, and for all over courses there is an increment in the percentage of growth rate. For the 1st period the annual growth rate was 5.96, 2.60, -4.28, and 1.16 for UG, PG, Engineering and Medical courses respectively which rose to 12.10, 12.53, 15.19 and 3.00 per cent in the 2nd period in respective terms. Against this there is an increase in engineering course's annual growth rate which has become 14.33 in 2nd period from 4.06 in the 1st period, while in all other courses there is decline and it is less than that of Scheduled Caste students in General courses like UG and PG where in 2nd period unreserved category is having enrolment of 1.74 and 3.68 respectively against 12.10 and 12.53 per cent annual growth rate of Scheduled Castes.

Gujarat—In Gujarat, annual growth rate of Scheduled Caste students is less compared to general students for the 2nd period however there is both increase and decrease in the rate for different courses from the level existed in 1st period i.e. between 1991 and 1997. In PG, Ph.D, Medical and Education courses, the annual growth rate is mere for General students vis-à-vis Scheduled Caste students from the 2nd period. The growth rate in these courses for General students is 12.22, 3.34, -0.06, and 14.10 respectively while for Scheduled Caste the rate of 10.15, 2.31, -1.00, and 14.06 per cent in respective terms.

Haryana—The annual enrolment rate for Haryana shows that though there is an increase in growth rate for 2nd period i.e. between 1997 and 2005 for both Scheduled Caste and General students in engineering course than existed in 1st period, however increase is more prominent for General students and which in total is 38.87 per cent while for Scheduled Caste it is 12.95 per cent. For PG, and medical courses, the decline has taken place for General as well as Scheduled Caste students, however such decline is more for Scheduled Caste students from the existent level in 1st period. In 1st period growth rate for Scheduled Caste in these courses was 21.97, and 15.30 respectively which in 2nd period become 8.17, and 8.04 for respective course, while for general students the existent rate in 1st period for these courses was 9.75, and 12.61 which become 8.18, and 8.95 per cent respectively for 2nd period.

Himachal Pradesh—In the state of Himachal Pradesh, there is decline in annual growth rate for Scheduled Caste students in 2nd period from 1st for Engineering and Education course while there is an increase in same for general students. In the 1st period growth rate for Scheduled Caste in these courses were 23.97 and 50.24 which declined to 20.51 and 26.34 per cent respectively in 2nd period. For General students growth rate for these courses were 23.87 and 13.25 per cent in 1st period which increased to 25.62 and 28.69 per cent in 2nd period. In the UG and medical course there is decline in growth rate both for General as well as Scheduled Caste students but the decline is more for Scheduled Caste students. The declare for general students in these courses was of 31 and 9 per cent respectively while for Scheduled Caste decline was of around 41 and 5 per cent in respective tens.

Karnataka—From the available figures it is visible that there is decline in annual growth rate of Scheduled Caste students in education course for the period between 1997 and 2005 when compared with level in period between 1991 and 1997, while on the reverse there is an increase in same for General students in same period of comparison. Growth rate between 1991 and 1997 for Scheduled Caste in Education course was 17.35 per cent which declared to -3.77 per cent in the 2nd period while for General student previous rate for education was -14.95 which increased 24 per cent to become 10.89 per cent in the 2nd period. In the Engineering course, the growth rate has increased both for general as well as for Scheduled Caste students however the rate has become more for Scheduled Caste students which is 16.72 in 2nd period in comparison to 10.59 per cent for General students.

Kerala—In Kerala, decline in growth rate is registered both for General and Scheduled Caste students in all courses except Engineering and Medical when growth rate for 2nd period is compared with that in 1st period. In engineering and medical course increase in growth rate is there for both categories however the increase is more for Scheduled Caste students where increment is of 46 and 12 per cent respectively against increase of 19 and 4 per cent for General students. In PG, Ph.D, and Education course decline is more for Scheduled Caste students which is of 13, 78, and 10 per cent in 2nd period from the level in 1st period while it is 10, 31, and 6 per cent decline for General students.

M.P. – In this state, the growth rate has increased and is better for Scheduled Caste students in comparison with general students in all courses of higher education as is reflected from the table and graph.

Maharashtra—In Maharashtra, there is decline on growth rate for enrolment of Scheduled Caste as well as of General students in all the courses except Engineering which has registered increase of 2 and 5 per cent point for respective category. In courses as P.G., Ph.D and Education, the growth rate for both categories has become negative for 2nd period.

Orissa—Figures of Orissa shows that there is decrease in growth rate for both general as well as SC category for 2nd period when compared to rate in 1st period for course of UG, Ph.D and Education. And there is increase in growth rate for both categories for engineering and medical course in the said period where the growth is more for SC with an increase of 27 and 7 per cent points in comparison to 16 and 4 per cent point increment for general students.

Punjab—In Punjab, increase in growth rate is registered for SC in course like PG, Ph.D, Engineer and Medical, when rate of 2nd Period (between 1997 and 2005) is compared with rate existed or 1st period (between 1991 and 1997). And there is decline in annual growth rate in UG and Education course. In general category, there is an increase in growth rate for Engineering, Ph.D and education courses for the said period. It is noteworthy that though there is increase in enrolment rate for both categories for engineering course, such increase is of 7 per cent point for general while of 1 per cent point for SC category.

Tamil Nadu—For the state of Tamil Nadu, there is increase in annual growth rate for both categories in PG, engineering, medical and Education courses in the period between 1997 and 2007 when compared with rates in between 1591 and 1997. While the growth is almost similar in the entire said course, there is more increase in enrolment rate of general students in engineering course in comparison to SC students. And annual growth rate for general students in period between 1997 and 2005 in engineering course of 31 per cent which was 5.58 in between 1991 and 1997, while for SC students it was 10.91 in between 1991 and 1997, which become 26.9 per cent in period between 1997 and 2005.

Tripura—In Tripura, figures for annual growth rate are not available for Ph.D and medical course. In the available figures, it can be said that there is declining trend for enrolment of SCs in all the courses. In engineering course there is decline of 7 per cent point in growth rate in 2nd period for 1st period for SC students while there is an increment of 10 per cent in the said period to reach 781 per cent in comparison to 2.34 per cent growth rate for SC has came down to 1 per cent for 20 per cent while for general students it has increased for –25.49 per cent to 38.14 per cent.

Uttar Pradesh—In U.P. (including Uttarakhand), there is steep increase in annual growth rate of SC students for 2nd period from 1st period in UG, engineering, medical and education course which has become 15.88, 98.77, 42.50 and 24.63 per cent respectively. While for general students it is 5.74, 22.32, 7.15 and 11.37 per cent respectively for 2nd period.

West Bengal—From the available figures, it is clear that there is increase in growth rate for SC students for all the courses except engineering where there is decline registered against increase in growth rate for general students. In engineering growth rate for SC students during period between 1991 and 1997 was 34.9 when it was –0.42 for general student. This growth rate for SC in period between 1997 and 2005 become 15.8 while it is 26.59 per cent for general students.

Chandigarh—Available data on Chandigarh makes it clear that there is increment in growth rate for SC students as well as for general students in various courses. However, major increase is registered for engineering with 31.79 and 41.60 per cent in general and SC students respectively for period between 1897 and 2005. Also increase is there for education course where the annual growth rate is of 7.78 and 6.81 per cent for general and SC students in the same period respectively. Earlier in period between 1991 and 1997 there was negative growth rate for both the categories in both courses.

Delhi—In Delhi, while there is increase in growth rate for SC students in all the courses, there is decline in growth rate for general students in UG, PG and Ph.D courses. In engineering, medical and education course, the growth rate for 2nd period for SC students is 27.02, 35.83 and 26.51 per cent respectively which has increased from –0.89, –20.63 and 0.91 per cent in 1st period. While for general students the growth rate for 2nd period for the said course is 17.15, 5.30 and 39.30 per cent.

Pondicherry—From the available figures, it can be said that there is decline in growth rate for all the courses except engineering for SC students while there is an increase in growth rate for general students for UG, engineering, medical and education course. In engineering course the growth registered in rate of enrolment for SC students of less i.e. of 8 points in comparison to 10 points increment for general students.

Having a glance over the table it becomes clear that there is increase in growth rate for SC students in all the courses at higher education however this increase is more prominent in engineering and medical courses which is 26.63 and 18.88 per cent respectively for period between 1997 and 2005 increasing from 11.64 and 7.80 in period between 1991 and 1997. In General category the growth rate has declined for UG and Ph.D. courses while it has increased for all other courses in period between 1997 and 2005 making a prominent increase in engineering course where the growth percentage is 21.18 an increase of 15 per cent from 6.34 in period between 1991 and 1997.

The tables make a comparison of Compound Annual Growth Rate between '1991 & 1997', and '1997 & 2005' for SCs and General students. From the available figures it can be said that the growth rate of SCs in all courses (in general) & in professional courses (in particular) is more in the period between 1997 & 2005. And this growth rate is more than the growth rate for general students.

The reasons for this may be assigned to their narrow base SC students were having previously especially in professional courses and some increment in figures leads to inflation in growth percentage. Also, the figures would have reflected the more number of repeaters in professional courses (Sinha, 2009) as their performance is bad at these courses (RCSCST 26th (1978-9)). Apart from the effective implementation of reservation policies, the growth in enrolment could be due to returns of education of 1st generation learners on the second generation learners who are enrolled. As if the parents are educated then 'community effect' which may hamper the educational as well as other development of child is negligible (Borooah & Iyer, 2002). This may reflect the concentration in participation at higher education by a hierarchical section of the entire SC community (Velaskar, 1986, Rao, 2000) and there is utilization and reutilization of reservation facilities by few caste(s) (Weisskopf, 2004).

From the tables, it can also be said that there are various states where the growth rate has either declined or is lower than that of general students in professional courses in particular, in the period between 1997 & 2005 when number of private colleges have increased, in comparison with the period between 1991 & 1997. These states are Assam, Haryana, Andhra Pradesh, Himachal Pradesh, Tamil Nadu, Tripura, West Bengal & Punjab which might be due to increase in number of private institutions in these states making it less affordable for SC students (Azad, 2004). Apart from error in data and anomalies in figures, which is possible explanation for huge inflation in enrolment of SC students in U.P. in engineering courses making growth of around 99 per cent, there is unavailability distinct data for different divisions in professional courses as engineering, etc. which might help in more comprehensive analysis of growth trend of SC students with general students.

The present data does not provide details about SCs participation in courses such as computer science, software, etc. which has became significant after liberalization era and are provided by private players which are dearly (Wankhede, 2003). Further the data is not available for the enrolled students who might have dropped out of the professional higher education system which is dearly for private institutions as economic backwardness and social stigma are major cause of students dropping out at higher education (Sinha, 1989). Most importantly the data of number of SC students enrolled in private institutions could clearly give the impact of privatization, which is unavailable.

4.3 Gross Enrolment Ratio among SC and General Category Students

This Table (4.5) is about GER of all students as well as of SC students in the age group of 18-24 in total higher education in different states of India in the year 2001 and 2005. Between the two years of comparison i.e. 2001 and 2005, GER of SC's has increased from 7.52 to 8.37, while that of All students has declined marginally from 12.4 to 11.55. In these two years, the GER of SC students has declined around 5.6, 0.19, 0.46, 0.59, 4.20, 0.26, 1.9, 19.31, 5.21, and 0.8 points for states of Assam, Bihar, Goa, Haryana, Himachal Pradesh, Jharkhand, Kerala, Maharashtra, Manipur, Orissa, and Uttarakhand respectively while it has increased for other states except west Bengal where it is constant at 5.02.among the states where the GER has increased to good amount with others, are Chhattisgarh, Gujarat, Sikkim, Tamil Nadu, Chandigarh (Union Territory), and Delhi with a difference of around 3.86, 3.90, 3.72, 2.36, 5.10, and 6.74 points respectively while data for states of Arunachal Pradesh, Meghalaya, Mizoram, Manipur, Nagaland, Andaman & Nicobar Islands, Daman & Diu, and Lakshadweep is unavailable.

GER of all categories show increase in states of Gujarat, Punjab, Andhra Pradesh, Sikkim, Tamil Nadu, Karnataka, Tripura,

Table 4.5: GER for SC and All Students

States/UTs	GER 2005 in Higher Education(18-24 years)			
	2001		2005	
	GER ALL	GER SC	GER ALL	GER SC
Andhra Pradesh	14.19	10.52	14.35	11.51
Arunachal Pradesh	7.01	4.59	7.19	-
Assam	15.28	11.31	6.80	5.74
Bihar	11.95	4.82	5.86	4.63
Chhattisgarh	8.91	8.13	8.69	11.99
Goa	14.96	9.96	13.05	9.50
Gujarat	8.94	8.2	10.14	12.10
Haryana	12.83	5.92	11.21	5.33
Himachal Pradesh	16.12	9.66	14.21	6.81
Jammu & Kashmir	12.58	5.19	12.56	6.97
Jharkhand	14.76	7.17	8.67	2.87
Karnataka	12.04	9.03	13.84	9.55
Kerala	17.6	10.8	11.57	10.54
Madhya Pradesh	8.92	5.4	13.77	13.52
Maharashtra	17.33	16.75	13.93	14.81
Manipur	33.37	33.77	12.64	14.46
Meghalaya	14.97	12.06	13.96	-
Mizoram	9	12.12	11.66	-
Nagaland	24.55	-	9.47	-
Orissa	13.66	8.37	9.34	3.16
Punjab	11.12	4.44	12.03	4.87
Rajasthan	8.23	4.77	7.41	5.06
Sikkim	6.24	4.13	11.98	7.85
Tamil Nadu	9.5	5.92	16.36	8.28
Tripura	6.24	5.2	6.50	6.24
Uttar Pradesh	12.57	7.29	9.29	8.71
Uttarakhand	17.81	9.51	15.74	8.73
West Bengal	8.63	5.02	8.21	5.02
A&N Islands	7.42	-	6.74	-
Chandigarh	26.67	10.37	41.41	15.47
D&N Haveli	3.3	8.92	0.00	-
Daman & Diu	3.91	10.34	3.96	-
Delhi	18.21	7.86	46.39	14.60
Lakshadweep	2.67	-	0.00	-
Puducherry	18.15	12.31	23.96	21.58
INDIA	12.4	7.52	11.55	8.37

Source: Selected Educational Statistics.

M.P, Andaman & Nicobar Islands, Mizoram, Chandigarh (Union Territory), Delhi, Pondicherry reflecting developed status with difference of 1.2, 0.91, 0.16, 5.74, 6.89, 1.80, 0.26, 4.85, 14.74, 2.66, 28.18, and 5.81 respectively, while major decline is registered in the states of Assam, Bihar, Jharkhand, Kerala, Maharashtra, Manipur, Nagaland, Orissa, U.P, Andaman & Nicobar Islands, Lakshadweep, with difference of 8.48,6.09,6.09,6.03, 3.4, 20.73,15.08, 4.32, 3.28, 3.3 and 2.67 respectively to reach at 6.80, 5.86, 8.67, 11.57, 13.93,12.64, 9.47, 9.34,9.29,0.00, and 0.00 in respective terms.

Table shows that GER of all students has declined marginally in the period between 2001 & 2005 when the number of private institutions providing higher education have increased the most (Anandkrishnan, 2006). In the SC category the GER for higher education has increased marginally in this period which might be due to the fact that ratio is gross and not net and therefore includes all age categories along with the repeaters (Sinha, 2009) in different courses. Also there might have possibility of inflated figures provided by some private institutions as a part of fulfilling the reservation norms. Finally, GER of SC students still lower than that of all students in higher education, & even such enrolment does not necessarily presents a favourable opinion about privatization as this might be due to well off families among SC students and majority of the SC population are still at bay from the arena of higher education (Velaskar, 1986, Rao, 2001).

Gender Parity Level among Scheduled Caste Students

After looking towards the enrolment trends, growth rate, and gross enrolment ratio for the scheduled caste students in higher education in India, there is a need to explore the facts about disparity that is existent within the SC category among the males and females across the disciplines at higher educational level.

This table (4.6) shows the growth in parity level from 1991 to 2005 in various courses at higher education level for Scheduled Caste girls' vis-à-vis their male counterparts. For the convenient

Table 4.6: Gender Parity among SC Students

		State	*AP*	*Assam*	*Bihar*	*Goa*	*Gujarat*	*Haryana*	*HP*	*J & K*	*Karnataka*	*Kerala*	*M P*	*Maharashtra*
1991	Gen. Edn.	UG	0.35	0.41	NA	0.56	0.48	0.12	0.22	0.25	0.27	1.10	0.18	0.31
		PG	0.22	0.51	NA	0.50	0.44	0.23	0.18	0.34	NA	0.87	0.25	0.23
		Ph.D	0.31	0.00	NA	NA	0.25	0.50	0.32	0.20	NA	0.43	0.45	0.49
	Prof. Edn.	Eng	0.06	0.08	NA	0.18	0.04	0.04	0.00	0.07	0.08	0.31	0.07	0.05
		Med	0.47	0.41	NA	1.80	0.38	0.29	0.21	0.71	0.47	0.85	0.29	0.61
		Edn	0.32	0.10	NA	NA	0.38	0.35	0.20	0.81	0.29	1.37	0.19	0.31
1997	Gen. Edn.	UG	0.48	0.53	0.10	1.10	0.21	0.38	0.59	NA	0.25	1.58	0.53	0.53
		PG	0.40	0.56	0.26	2.00	0.75	0.51	0.50	NA	0.15	1.87	0.78	0.43
		Ph.D	0.20	0.67	0.39	0.60	0.52	0.25	0.31	NA	0.19	0.97	1.25	0.22
	Profe	Eng	0.39	0.21	0.07	0.27	0.19	0.14	0.20	NA	0.41	0.65	0.20	NA
		Med	0.97	0.39	0.20	1.80	0.50	0.20	0.35	NA	0.62	1.90	0.61	0.91
		Edn	0.39	0.43	0.34	1.00	0.60	1.09	0.33	NA	0.42	2.13	0.27	0.38
2005	Gen. Edn.	UG	0.51	0.52	0.12	1.10	0.58	0.65	0.82	0.90	0.63	1.78	0.69	0.75
		PG	0.57	0.65	0.17	0.64	1.02	0.63	0.95	0.99	0.58	2.38	0.75	0.66
		Ph.D	0.35	5.00	0.30	NA	0.66	0.41	0.66	0.89	0.60	1.00	0.47	0.26
	Profe	Eng	0.28	0.40	0.14	0.48	0.19	0.17	0.24	0.24	0.68	1.62	0.34	0.32
		Med	0.61	0.28	0.62	1.11	0.68	0.65	0.61	0.92	0.90	1.65	0.71	0.93
		Edn	0.70	1.55	0.03	1.00	0.80	0.78	1.02	1.25	0.76	4.69	0.73	0.82

(Contd.)

Table 4.6 *(contd.)*

		State	*Orissa*	*Punjab*	*Rajasthan*	*T.N.*	*Tripur*	*U P*	*W B*	*Chandi*	*Delhi*	*Pondi*	*India*
1991	Gen. Edn.	UG	0.19	0.62	0.05	0.46	0.34	0.07	0.47	0.45	0.57	0.33	0.31
		PG	0.28	0.60	0.04	0.38	0.70	0.09	0.41	0.43	0.55	0.31	0.22
		Ph.D	0.27	0.58	0.20	0.25	NA	0.13	0.53	NA	0.31	NA	0.29
	Profe	Eng	0.02	0.04	NA	0.13	0.08	0.03	0.04	0.02	0.09	0.38	0.09
		Med	0.38	0.48	NA	0.71	NA	0.14	0.11	NA	0.91	0.46	0.50
		Edn	0.44	0.87	NA	1.27	0.08	0.20	0.09	2.24	2.94	1.86	0.36
1997	Gen. Edn.	UG	0.33	1.00	0.15	0.66	0.76	0.27	0.51	0.74	0.75	1.06	0.42
		PG	0.48	1.43	0.14	0.62	0.62	0.34	0.50	0.76	0.52	0.52	0.47
		Ph.D	0.76	NA	0.37	0.50	0.00	0.28	0.57	1.14	0.27	0.47	0.36
	Profe	Eng	0.16	0.18	0.37	0.33	0.17	0.39	0.09	0.27	0.24	0.44	0.34
		Med	0.63	1.22	0.26	0.59	0.35	0.32	0.11	1.39	1.06	1.51	0.70
		Edn	0.66	1.65	0.50	1.05	1.27	0.23	0.82	6.00	0.86	2.08	0.56
2005	Gen. Edn.	UG	0.32	0.99	0.34	0.87	0.66	0.57	0.53	1.21	0.95	0.90	0.59
		PG	0.24	1.71	0.40	0.98	0.81	0.36	0.44	0.79	0.99	0.95	0.55
		Ph.D	0.52	0.60	0.15	0.61	NA	0.48	0.27	1.14	0.57	0.54	0.47
	Profe	Eng	0.85	0.21	0.12	0.46	0.26	0.08	0.16	0.24	0.17	0.34	0.36
		Med	0.22	1.58	0.41	1.42	0.47	0.57	0.73	2.00	1.40	1.01	0.86
		Edn	0.54	2.72	0.61	2.35	0.83	0.46	0.33	3.00	1.33	1.30	0.68

Source: Selected Educational Statistics.

study of the growth in parity in all the states of India for fourteen years, the parity level is seen for three different years i.e. 1991, 1997, and 2005, which will cover the full period and also impact of growth of private colleges can be seen.

Under-graduate Courses

For the year 1991, majority of the states are having parity level between 0.25 and 0.50 followed by the states having parity below 0.25, and least number of states had parity level between 0.51 and 0.75. States with parity level between 0.25 and 0.50 are Andhra Pradesh, Assam, Gujarat, Jammu A Kashmir, Karnataka, Maharashtra, Tamil Nadu, Tripura, West Bengal, Chandigarh (Union Territory), and Pondicherry (Union Territory). Also, India as a whole was having a parity of 0.31 for Scheduled Caste girls. Goa, Punjab, and Delhi (National Capital Territory) were having parity level between 0.51 and 0.75 while below 0.25 level parity existed in states like Haryana, Himachal Pradesh, Madhya Pradesh, Orissa, Rajasthan, and U.P. showing low participation of women in these states in Under Graduate courses. This lowest parity continued in 1997 for Bihar, Gujarat, and Rajasthan while Andhra Pradesh, Haryana, Orissa, and U.P. were having parity level between 0.25 and 0.50 in 1997.

However the highest parity level was in Kerala which was having parity of 1.10 in 1991 which increased to 1.58 in 1997 and to 1.78 in 2005. Kerala was followed by Chandigarh with parity level of 1.21 in 2005. Apart from this, states with parity level between 0.75 and 1.20 in 2005 are Himachal Pradesh, Jammu & Kashmir, Tamil Nadu, Pondicherry, Delhi, Goa, and Punjab. However parity level for India as a whole in 2005 has reached to 0.59 showing disparity.

Post-graduate Courses

In the PG courses, the parity level of scheduled caste girls for India has risen from 0.22 in 1991 to 0.47 in 1997 which in 2005 has reached to 0.55. While the parity level varies in different states, the lowest parity is seen in states like U.P, Rajasthan, Himachal Pradesh, Andhra Pradesh, and Haryana for 1991 with level of 0.09, 0.04, 0.18, 0.22, and 0.23 which rose to 0.36, 0.40, 0.95, 0.57, and 0.63 in 2005 respectively. Apart from this, Kerala is the state with highest parity since 1991 when the level was 0.87 which rose to 1.87 in 1997 and finally 2.38 is the parity level in 2005. Rest all the states are lying in the category where the parity level is 0.51 and 0.75 except some states like Himachal Pradesh, Tripura, Chandigarh (union territory), and Pondicherry (Union Territory) where the parity level for PG courses in Schedules Caste category is near to one.

Ph.D Courses

In 1991, the parity level for scheduled caste girls for Ph.D course was 0.29 at India level which rose to 0.36 in 1997 and finally reached 0.47 in 2005 showing double participation of girls in this course for the level of 1991. Majority of the states in 1991 were having the parity between 0.25 and 0.50 which remained same for 1997 however in 2005the parity level increased to level between 0.51 and 0.75 which was having in majority of states as Andhra Pradesh, Assam, Goa, Haryana Karnataka, Madhya Pradesh and Maharashtra. Between 1997 and 2005, the states which have achieved psrity are M.P, Assam, Kerala, and Chandigarh (Union Territory).

Professional Courses

In these courses, parity level was low in 1991 at 0.09 for **Engineering** course which rose to 0.34 in 1997, and 0.36 in 2005 with a marginal increase at all India level. In 1991 majority of the states were having parity below 0.25 for engineering course including Andhra Pradesh, Assam, Goa, Gujarat, Haryana, Himachal Pradesh, Jammu & Kashmir, Karnataka, M.P, Maharashtra, Orissa, Punjab, Tamil Nadu, Tripura, U.P, West Bengal, Chandigarh (union territory) and Delhi (National Capital Territory). The parity level of majority of states changed to level between 0.25 and 0.50 for 1997 and continued till 2005, except low parity below 0.25 in Bihar, Gujarat, Haryana, Himachal Pradesh, Jammu & Kashmir, Punjab, Rajasthan, U.P, West Bengal, Chandigarh (Union Territory), and Delhi (National Capital Territory). The state which has achieved parity for engineering course during the course of time is Kerala with level of 1.62.

For the Medical course parity level for India in 1991 was 0.50 which rose to 0.70 in 1997 and finally in 2005 reached to 0.86. While majority of the states including Andhara Pradesh, Assam, Gujarat, Haryana, Karnataka, M.P, Orissa, Punjab, and Pondicherry were having parity between 0.25 and 0.50 in 1991, there were states like Delhi, Goa, Jammu & Kashmir, Maharashtra, And Tamil Nadu where the parity level was between 0.51 and more than 1,20. In 1997, around 13 states were having parity level between 0.51 an above 1.20 while only Bihar, Haryana, West Bengal were having parity below 0.25 for Scheduled Caste girls. The parity level further improved in 2005 when five states i.e. Kerala, Punjab, Tamil Nadu, Chandigarh (Union Territory) and Delhi (National Capital Territory) are having parity level above 1.20 while five states are in category of parity level between 0.76 an 1.20.

In the Education course, the parity level for India in 1991 was 0.36 rising to 0.56 in 1997 and to 0.68 in 2005. In 1991 six states were lying in parity level between 0.25 and 0.50 while states like Punjab, Kerala, Tamil Nadu, Chandigarh (Union Territory), Delhi (National Capital Territory), and Pondicherry (Union Territory) have achieved parity. In 1997 the number of states achieved parity were eight while still majority of the states were holding previous parity level except U.P. which is having the lowest parity below 0.25. The number of states in 2005 which has either achieved parity or is near to the same in education in Education were thirteen while six states including U.P, West Bengal, Andhra Pradesh, M.P, Orissa, and Rajasthan were having parity between 0.25 and 0.75. And Bihar is at the last with parity of 0.03.

From the table it becomes clear that though the level of disparity in Scheduled Caste girls' enrolment in various courses has declined since 1991 still achievement of parity level is far from reality for all courses except Medical where the level was better in 1991 and continued to better with a continuous rise. Apart from this none of the courses at all India level has shown extensive growth towards achievement of parity and the figures for Engineering course is really very low requiring attention. The growth in Engineering in particular is dismal despite coming of large number of private colleges to impart this course.

The parity table of SC girls in higher education makes it conspicuous that between the periods of study i.e. From 1991 to 2005, there is no significant growth in enrolment of girls at various courses of higher education. However the growth has certainly taken place which is possible due to extreme low base of girls in terms of enrolment in higher education. Participation in education by SC girls is not effective at lower levels of education vis-à-vis their male counterparts. This results in dropping out of girls from education system at different levels (Chitnis, 1989).

Further social stigma is a major cause behind their dropping out of higher education system (Sinha, 1989). It is noteworthy that though the growth has taken place in terms of SC girls' enrolment in higher education, such growth is restricted to general courses and in medical and education course at professional level reflecting social stereotypical attitude towards them where they are supposed to be fit for soft subjects and therefore their participation is dismal in engineering courses. Among the states, Kerala, Punjab, Chandigarh (Union Territory), Tamil Nadu, and Delhi (National Capital Territory) have registered a significant enhancement in the participation of SC women, which might be due to educational advancement of these states and also industrialization in these states might have paved for their participation in higher education.

Conclusion

Higher education always had an important role in the growth of an individual's personality as well as for a state's development and as therefore its level is an indicator of State's development having a direct relationship with it (Verghese, 2001). The role of higher education has become much more significant in the present age of knowledge economy and therefore need is to universalize higher education by making it more inclusive and democratic (Verghese, 2001).

From the present study it was found that if we look at the enrolment trend among SC students who are deprived both economically and socially, the trend which emerges is their growth in terms of enrolment in various general as well as professional courses (see table enrolment) which is the resultant of implementation of various 'affirmative action' in terms of reservation policies in the existing universities and its affiliated colleges where reservation policies are still existent and in the states where large number of private institutions are coming in, the enrolment percent might have declined, however exact data having such details is unavailable.

Regarding their comparison with General students, though growth has taken place for the former due to their narrow base in the previous years and slight change would get magnified. And in absolute terms the change is not that prominent. Also, coming of private colleges has not tackled the disparity of SC girls in higher education and their position continues to be dismal except some industrially developed states (see table 4.9). In the present study it is shown that the disparity among male and females of the SC category is more in the professional courses like engineering where except Kerala with parity level of 1.62, all the stases are lagging behind. In terms of GER, total SC population is at the lowest pedestal (Thorat, 2009).

Privatization without any restrictions would result in commercialization where the profit will be the sole motive of the investor (Tilak, 1999). This will contribute to the persistence of socio-economic inequalities in the society providing elitist bias in education (Kaul, 1990). It has been argued by the pro-pounders of privatization that for economically deprived students facilities will be to provide loan to meritorious students, however due to structural as well as administrative constraints it is not workable and therefore not acceptable (Tilak, 1997). Further SC is not only an economically deprived community but is socially discriminated albeit not in theory. Also, the need for developed status of the state is to universalize Higher education instead of restricting it to few. It can be said that privatization of higher education will be a disaster for SC students as thereafter reservation clause of constitution to establish equity won't hold true.

Above all, there are social returns attached to higher education along with private returns which are falling over time (Tilak, 1997). In a developing nation like India higher education is having social returns of about 11 per cent (Psacharopoulous and Patrinos, 2002). And reservation at higher education is basically an effort to promote integration of upper strata of society by increasing access to the disadvantaged to the elite persons (Weisskopf, 2004).

In sum, privatization of higher education would lead to stunted growth of the state as mass will remain outside the ambit of higher education which will become dearly (Jayaram, 2004).

5

Effective Monitoring and Implementation of Reservation Policy (Conclusion)

The role of higher education has become much more significant in the present century. This is due to the enhanced role of knowledge driven society in the present world to have real development (Verghese, 2001). Higher education is an important factor in creating knowledge base in the society. In the last decade of the 20th century the world has become more globalised than it had been in the previous centuries. As a result the phenomenon of 'privatization' has intruded in all the sectors of economy of the state.

In India, privatization in higher education is initiated following the guidelines of World Bank which has accepted higher education as a commodity with less social returns and therefore less state's assistance and control is required. This has led for establishment of more number of private aided and unaided institutions offering higher education in India albeit the number of 'unfettered privatization' where each component of higher education in the institution(s) is privately decided is still less. More number of privately owned and managed higher educational institutions will impact negatively on the democratization process of higher education as now it will be concentrated into the hands of the students whose family could afford it.

In such a scenario where the state's welfare role in terms of furthering higher education which is attractive and affordable to all, is restricted, the participation of SC students in higher education gets double disadvantage in the form of economic deprivation and social discrimination. This will also dismiss the constitutional commitment to undo the backwardness of SCs as the reservation clause which is provided as an instrument of protective discrimination, will collapse under unrestricted privatization in higher education.

In this context the present study was conducted with three fold motives. Firstly the study analyzed the phenomenon of 'privatization' in higher education in India. Secondly, to have glance at the impact of privatization in Indian higher education since 1991, the enrolment trends of SC students in various courses at different levels was noticed and compared with that of General category students. Finally the impact of privatization of higher education was seen on establishing parity among the SC category.

Key terms utilized in the present study were Higher Education, Scheduled Castes, and Privatization. In the study the term 'higher education' implied education that is imparted after the senior secondary stage. Though the term 'higher education' encapsulates varied disciplines and courses, however for this study the higher education will include general education i.e. science, commerce, and arts streams at under and professional education i.e. engineering, medical, and education at various levels. Term Scheduled Castes in the study meant castes those have traditionally been relegated to the most menial labour with no possibility of upward mobility and are subject to extensive social disadvantage and discrimination by the other categories of 'chaturvarna system' in 1935 the British passed the Government of India act which brought the term 'scheduled caste' into use and comprised various castes, races or tribes, which were formerly under the category of depressed class. As per the 2001 census the population is over 16 per cent. These had been provided by the constitution safeguard in the form of reservation of 15 per cent in all public institutions and authorities. Finally 'privatization' was used in higher education to define aided, unaided, and unrestricted institutions (Chalam, 2004).

The specific objectives of the study were: (a) To analyze the various government policies mentioned in NPE'86, 92 and in various Five Year Plans about the higher education and its impact on SC students, (b) To study the enrolment pattern of SCs in both general and professional higher education, (c) To study the existing gap between SC and General category students in terms of enrolment in higher education in different courses at various levels in different states of India, and (d) To study the gender difference among the SC category in higher education.

The present study was descriptive in nature.

The study was conducted by using secondary data only. Secondary data were sourced from various documents such as U.G.C. Annual Report, Annual Report (MHRD), Selected Educational Statistics, and National Sample Survey Organization (NSSO) for analyzing enrolment of SCs in higher education. To analyze the 'Privatization' in Indian higher education system on the ground of feasibility from the aspect of legal provisions, social equity, and political aspirations, critical review of various government policies on higher education and in various five year plans was done by the investigator. Information was also collected from various books, articles, research papers and unpublished dissertation and theses.

The important findings of the study may be summarized into four

(i) the phenomenon of privatization is there in Indian higher education and the complete or unrestricted privatization is increasing,

(ii) analysis of various policy documents made it clear that there is no conspicuous and distinct mention about higher educational interests of SC students,

(iii) enrolment trends shows that there is an increase in enrolment of SCs in higher education, however they are still lagging behind in comparison to the General and other category students,

(iv) coming of privatization has not undone the gender disparity among SCs as they are still far behind their male counterparts in higher education.

Regarding the enrolment of SCs in higher education, it comes out the study that there has not been significant increase in GER of the SC category at higher education while there is decline in enrolment of all students from 12.4 in 2001 to 11.55 in 2005 which is also shown in GER table where their GER is 8 while that of all students is 12 in the year 2005. This growth among SCs from 7.52 in 2001 is marginal and that too is seen in few states as Delhi (N.C.T.), Chandigarh (U.T.), Pondicherry (U.T), A.P., Sikkim, and U.P. where industrial advancement is more or due to various other factors such as inflated figures, more number of repeaters, effective implementation of reservation policies, effective cells in the institutions, so on and forth. And the decline among all students symbolizes the ill effects of privatization in higher education.

Though there is an enhancement in the enrolment in professional courses among the SC category, such an enhancement is not a reflector of the increased participation of SC students in total (democratized participation) rather it might be the result of more number of repeaters in the course(s) which is allowed in the private colleges and is affordable to few concentrated sections among SC category. Also, such growth is the result of the narrow base this category was having in higher education. This can be said on the basis of results found out from the study which reveals that their enrolment is still far less than their actual population in the state(s) except Goa, where the participation of SCs is more than their population however the state has registered a decline in their enrolment percentage in 2005 when compared with the level of percent share in 1997. There are various states which has registered decline in most of the courses particularly in professional education (where the privatization is seen maximum) as Delhi (N.C.T.), Gujarat, Chandigarh (U.T.), Rajasthan, A.P. (in Engineering), M.P., and Pondicherry (U.T.).

As far as gender parity among the SC category is concerned though it has increased in some of the courses in higher education such an increase has not established the parity level of one. There is not much increase in the course as arts, medical and education which is supposed fit for women and the level was almost the same in 2005. And there is decline in some of these courses from the parity level it has achieved in the previous years as in medical and education course in different states as Pondicherry (U.T.), Kerala, A.P., Goa, H.P., Tripura, Chandigarh (U.T.), and Delhi (N.C.T.). Over all there is some increase in enrolment of SC girls which has reduced some disparity but this growth is not prominent to establish parity or in reaching near the parity level as shown in parity table except some industrially and educationally advanced states as Kerala, Delhi (N.C.T.), Chandigarh (U.T.), Pondicherry (U.T.), Assam, H.P., and T.N. where parity level has been achieved or is near to achievement. In case of professional course of engineering their parity level far from satisfactory in any state of the nation except Kerala where it is 1.62.

The study conducted reveals that the privatization has been favoured under the policies, programs, and plans of Indian governments since the last decade of the 20th century however the unrestricted private institutions are still less in numbers. This has impacted negatively the students pursuing higher education as now the entire share of pursuing higher education would be borne by the consumer or student. The impact of unrestricted private institutions will be much more detrimental in the case of SC students as the reservation clause as a safeguard provided to them by the Constitution of India would be of no use and their participation will reduce except some of its well off sections which can afford it. The phenomenon of privatization of higher education will be further negative in terms of establishing gender parity among the SC category as there exists social stigma against the investment in girl's education and in the wake of no incentives in the form of scholarships, hostel facilities, special cells, etc. their participation level might have reduce in the coming years when there will be dominance of unfettered private higher education in India.

Current trends of higher educational enrollments of the Scheduled Caste (SC) students in particular shows that they are mainly concentrated at (now) low esteemed courses like that of Arts, and not in more globally demanded courses as that of Engineering, etc. technical courses. The reason for such a dismal scenario could be varied. One alarming yet satisfying explanation could be explored at the elementary and secondary level of SC students' education, source of their limited capability forcing them to be restricted at certain (impervious) boundary of a discipline.

Long time has already elapsed since Indian policy planners (to the tune of globalized norms) are concerned about quality issues in education and particularly for equality of opportunity in education. Not to our surprise, there has been severe shortfall between proposals made and realization achieved at this front. There lies a great deal of merit in noting down that ideal of 'meritocracy' (we are striving for) remain a farce till the time we won't learn to democratize (emphasizing inclusion) our school education system. In the system which tend to maintain and reproduce (elite) cultural habitus, either drop out (on various counts) of socially and culturally disadvantaged groups could be anticipated or at the most (in case of continuation) there are limited clientele group (Eligible Enrolment Ratio, EER) available to pursue professional courses at higher education level.

Implications

The present study has analyzed the phenomenon of 'privatization' in higher education in India and its implication on the enrolment trends of SCs in different states of the country. On the basis of results found the different policy implications for the study are as follows:

- Policies are required to have more allocation of funds for higher education keeping unfettered privatization at bay. This will enhance the enrolment and participation of all the students and particularly of SC students in higher education.
- There is need for effective implementation of available reservation policies for better participation of students belonging to SC category in higher education.
- To have more number of SC students in higher education the requirement is to have policies that ensure better

participation at school level which acts as a base for higher education.

- There is requirement to have more number of freeships and scholarships to the SC students in higher education in general and in professional education in particular.
- In order to have parity among the SCs in different disciplines in higher education special ear marked policies for SC girls' participation at all levels is needed to be brought in.
- Adequate hostel facilities ensuring residence to all SC students in general and of SC girls in particular who are pursuing higher education away from their home town are required, to have their enhanced participation from remote locations in institutions of higher learning.
- Policies to establish more number of public institutions offering quality higher learning are required to have enhanced choices for SCs to pursue higher education.
- Special cells for SC students in the institutions of higher learning has a positive effect on the participation of the same and therefore such cells are required to be established in all the institutions with effective monitoring by higher authorities.
- In case of giving permit to establish private institutions the governing body should ensure that reservation clause and other incentives provided to the SC students does not collapse.
- In order to have better analysis of the enrolment trends of SCs the basic requirement is to have a database which is comprehensive in nature and captures the data distinctly for different disciplines in higher education.
- Apart from all these, there is a requirement to establish direct linkage of all the available disciplines with the jobs to have better enrolment in the same.
- Above all, it is equally important to have database capturing the existing reality of women's participation in different disciplines of higher learning.

References

Abbasayulu, Y.B. (1978) *Scheduled Caste Elite: A Study of Scheduled Caste elite in Andhra Pradesh*, Hyderabad, Department of Sociology, Osmania University.

Agarwal, P. (2007) Higher Education in India: Growth, Concerns, and Change Agenda, *Higher Education Quarterly*, vol. 61 no. 2, pp. 197-207.

Aggarwal and Sibou (1994) *Educating Scheduled Castes: A study of inter district and intra caste differentials*, NIEPA, New Delhi.

Aggarwal, V. and Sharma, R.U. (2004) Privatization vs. Commercialization of Higher Education: Some Facts, Concerns and Suggestions, *University News* 42(7), pp. 25-28.

Aikara, J. (1980) Scheduled Castes and Higher Education: A Study of College Students in Bombay, Dastane Ramchandra and Co., Poona-2.

Akhoury, R. (2008) Impact of Globalization on Dalits, in Thakur, A. K. and Thakur, R. N. (Ed.) *Impact of Economic Reform Policies on Dalit and Weaker Sections*, Deep and Deep publications, New Delhi.

Altbach, P. G (1999) Private Higher Education: Themes and Variations in Comparative Perspective, *Prospects*, vol. 29 (3) Sept. 1999, pp. 310-323.

Ambani, M. and Birla, M.K. (2002) A Policy Framework for Reforms in Education, the Report Submitted to PMCTI on Apr.24.

Ambrose, P. (2000) Globalization and the Changing Ideology of Indian Higher Education, *Social Action*, vol. 50, October-December.

Anandkrishnan (2006) Privatization of Higher Education: Opportunities and Anomalies. paper presented in the national seminar on 'Privatization and Commercialization of Higher Education' organized by NIEPA, New Delhi on May2, 2006 In Prakash, V. 2007. Trends in Growth and Financing of Higher Education in India. *Economic and Political Weekly*, August 2, 2007: 3249-3258.

Astin, A. W. (1999) Student Involvement: A Developmental Theory for Higher Education, *Journal of College Student Development*, vol. 40 no. 40, pp. 518-529.

Astin, A.W. and Leticia, O. (2004) The Declining "Equity" of American Higher Education, *The Review of Higher Education*, vol. 27(3), pp. 321-341.

Azad, J.L. (2004) Privatization of Higher Education. *University News* 42(07): 19-24.

Azam, M. and Blom, A. (2008) Progress in Participation in Tertiary Education in India from 1983 to 2004. Policy Research Working Paper No. 4793, The World Bank South Asian Region, Human Development Department, December, 2008.

Bakshi, P.M. (2004) *Constitution of India*, Universal Publishers, New Delhi.

Barik, R. K.(2012) *Reviewing the Reservation Policy in Changing Social Order*, Shipra Publications, Delhi.

Barooah, V. K. and Iyer, S. (2002) Vidya, Veda, and Varna: The Influence of Religion, and Caste on Education in Rural India, Research Paper-International Centre for Economic Research, Torino, United Kingdom.

Basant, R. (2008) Decoding Access, *Seminar*, Jul, pp. 19-22.

Bhatt, G.D. (2005) *Educational Development of Scheduled Castes, Himalayan Region Study and Research Institute*, Delhi, pp. 49-97.

Bourdieu, P. (1974) 'The School as a Conservative Force: Scholastic and Cultural Inequalities' In John Eggleston (Ed.) (1974) *Contemporary Research Sociology of Education*, London: Methuen p. 37.

Bowen, H. (1980) *Investment in Lerning: The Individual and Social Value of American Higher Education*, Jossey-Bass Publishers, San Francisco.

Bray, M. (2000) Education in Asia: Financing Higher Education, *Prospects*, vol. 30(3), pp. 331-348.

Castells, M. (1991) Universities as Dynamic Systems of Contradictory Functions' In Muller, Cloete and Badat (ed.) (2001) *Challenges of Globalization South African Debates with Manuel Castells. Centres for Higher Education Transformation*. Maskew Miller Longman Ltd. Cape Town.

Census of India (2002), Primary Census Abstract: Census of India 2001. New Delhi: Government of India.

Chakrabarti, Anindita (2009); 'Determinants of Participation in Higher Education and Choices of Disciplines: Evidence from Urban and Rural Indian Youth', *South Asia Economic Journal*, 10(2), pp. 371-402.

Chalam, K. S. (2004) Privatization of Higher Education Under WTO Regime, *University News*, 42(07), 16-24.

Chalam, K.S. (1988) *Education and the Weaker Sections*, Inter India Publications, New Delhi.

Chalam, K.S. (2008) Higher Education For Dalits After Globalization, in *Modernization and Dalit Education: Ambedkar's Vision*, Rawat Publications, Jaipur.

Chatterjee, S.K. (2000) Educational Development and Social Integration, in *Educational Development of Scheduled Castes: Looking Ahead*, Gyan Publishing House, New Delhi, pp. 269-291.

Chattopadhyay, S. (2007) Exploring Alternative Sources of Financing Higher Education, *Economic and Political Weekly*, 20th October.

Chauhan, C.P.S. (2004) Privatization of higher Education : A Socio- Economic Perspectives, *University News* 42 (07) Feb,16-22, pp. 35-39.

Chitins, S. (1976) Problems of the Scheduled Caste College Students of Bombay, Tata Institute of Social Science, Bombay.

Chitins, S. (1981) A Long Way To Go....Report on a Survey of SC high School and College Students in 15 States of India, Allied Publishers, New Delhi.

Choudhary, K. (1998) Dalits in Higher Education: Cooption or Domination, *Journal of Higher Education*, 21(3), pp. 437-52.

Choudhary, S. K. (2008) Higher Education of India: A Socio- Historical Journey for Ancient Period to 2006-07, *Journal of Educational Enquiry*, Vol. 8 no. 1.

Crosnoe, R., Mistry, S. R. and Elder, H. Glen,Jr.(2002) Economic Disadvantage, Family Dynamics and Adoloescent Enrolment in Higher Education. *Journal of Marriage and Family,* Vol. 64, pp. 690-702.

Desai, S. and Kulkarni, V. (2008) 'changing Educational Inequalities in India in the Context of Affirmative Action', *Demography*, vol. 45 no. 2 (May), pp. 245-70 .

Deshpande, S. and Yadav, Y. (2006) Redesigning Affirmative Action- Castes and Benefits in Higher Education, *Economic and Political Weekly* 17th June, pp. 2419-2424.

Deshpande, S. (2008) Sharing Social Composition, *Seminar,* July.

Dixon, P. and Tooley, M. (2006) Defacto Privatization of Education and the Poor: Implication of a Study from Sub-Saharan Africa and India, *Compare* 36(04) pp. 443-462

FICCI Survey; http// www.ficci.com/press/06031pasurveyoneducation .doc

Ghosh, J. (2006) Case for Caste based Quotas in Higher Education, *Economic and Political Weekly*, 17th June, pp. 2428-2432.

Ghosh, J. (2008) Caste and Discrimination in Higher Education: Evidence from the National Sample Surveys, paper for Conference on Affirmative Action in Higher Education in India, the United States and South Africa, New Delhi, 19-21March, 2008.

GOI (1966) Report of the Education Commission (1964-66), Ministry of Education, Government of India, New Delhi.

GOI (Various years) Analysis of Budgeted Expenditure on Education, MHRD, New Delhi.

Gorettilourdes, G. R. (2002) Academic Achievement of the Scheduled Caste College Students in Manonmaniam Sundaranar University , *The Indian Journal of Social Work,* vol. 63 (4), pp. 540-551.

Government of India (1990) *Towards an Enlightened and Humane Society.* Ramamurthy Committee Report for Review of National Policy on Education 1986.

Gupta, A. (2005) International Trends in Private Higher Education and the Indian Scenario, Research and Occasional Paper Series (CSHE.11.05), Centre for Studies in Higher Education, University of California, Berkeley.

Halsey, H.A. Et al.(Ed.) (1997) *Education Culture, Economy and Society*, Oxford University Press, London.

Iliah, K. (2006) Merit of Reservations, *Economic and Political Weekly*, 17 June.

Jain, A. K, and Moni, N. (1987) Importance of Female Primary Education For Fertility Reduction in India, in Ghosh, R. and Zachariah, M. (ed.) *Education and the Process of Change*, Sage publications, New Delhi.

James, Richard (2002). Socio-economic Background and Higher Education Participation: An analysis of School Students' aspirations and expectations. Commonwealth of Australia.

Jayaram, N. (2004) Higher Education in India: Massification and Change, in Philip G. Altbach and Toru Umakoshi (ed.) *Asian Universities Historical Perspectives and Contemporary Challenges*, Johns Hopkins University, Baltimore.

Jogidand P.G. (2007) Development of Dalits, *Indian Journal of Social Work*, 1 January, pp. 57-72.

Kale, R.K. (2008) Enrolling or Rolling Out: SC and ST students in Central Universities, *University News*, 46(22), June2-8

Kamat, R.A. (1989) Education and Social Change: A Conceptual Framework, in Singh, A. and Sharma, D.G. (Ed.) *Higher Education in India: The Social Context*, Konark Publishers, Delhi.

Kaul, R. (1993) *Caste, Class and Education: Politics of the Capitation Fee Phenomenon in Karnataka*, Sage Publications, New Delhi.

Kinjaram, R. (1998) *Educational Performance of Scheduled Castes*, AP- Publishing House, New Delhi.

Kirpal, V. and Gupta, M. (1999) Equality Through Reservations, (Jaipur: Rawat), In Basant, Rakesh and Sen Gitanjali (2009) Who Participates in Higher Education in India? Rethinking the Role of Affirmative Action, working paper no. 2009-11-01, Nov. 2009.

Kirpal, V. (1985) Wastage among Scheduled Caste and Scheduled Tribe Students, *Journal of Higher Education*, 11, pp. 111-16.

Kumar, A. (2004) Higher Education in India: The Contemporary Challenges Facing it, Paper presented at the workshop on 'Challenges in Higher Education Today', University of Pune, 2004.

Lahoti, R. C. (2004) *Preamble: The spirit and backbone of the Constitution of India* 2, Eastern Book Co., Lucknow.

Levy, D. C. (2008) Private Higher Education: Patterns and Trends, *New Frontiers in Education*, vol. 41, no. 1.

Lynch, K. (2001) Equality in Education, *An Irish Quarterly Review.* Vol. 90, No. 360 (Winter), pp. 399-411.

Mahadeva, M. (2003) Critical Reflection on Development of Scheduled Castes, *Journal of Social and Economic Development*, Jan-June, pp. 17-39.

Majumdar, T. (1983) Investment in Education and Social Choice. Cambridge: Cambridge University Press. In Tilak, J.B.G. (2004) Public Subsidies in Education in India. *Economic and Political Weekly.* Vol. 39(4): 343-359.

Malhotra, N. and Rizvi, N. (1997) S*ource Material on Education of SCs and STs,* Anamika Publishers, Delhi.

Malik, S. (1979) *Social Integration of Scheduled Caste*, Abhinav Publications, New Delhi.

Mandelsohn, O. and Vicziamy, M. (1998) *The Untouchables: Subordination, Poverty and the State in Modern India*, Cambridge University Press, Cambridge, United Kingdom.

Mannivannan, D.G. (2004) The Implications of GATS Trade in Higher Education Services: The Indian Perspective of Private Participation, *University News* 42(07) Feb.16-22.

Mehta, A. and Hasan, R (2006) Under representations of Disadvantaged Classes in Colleges- what do data tell us?, *Economic and Political Weekly*, 2 September.

Mehta, B. P. and Kapur, D. (2004) Indian Higher Education Reform: From Half Baked Socialism to Half Bake Capitalism, Centre for International Development Working Paper no. 108.

Mehta, B. P. (2006) Democracy, disagreement and Merit, *Economic and Political Weekly*, June 17, pp. 2425-2427.

Mehta, B.C. (1993) Financing of Higher Education, *Journal of Educational Planning and Administration*, Vol. vii no. 1, January.

Mehta, P.B. (2006) Democracy, Disagreement and Merit, *Economic and Political Weekly* June 17, pp. 2425-2427.

Mingat, A. and Peng T. J. (1996) The Full Social Return to Education: Estimates Based on Countries' Economic Growth Performance, Human Capital Development Working Paper No. 73, Washington D.C : World Bank.

Ministry of Human Resource Development (Various Years) Selected Educational Statistics, Government of India, New Delhi.

——(Various Years) Annual Report, Government of India, New Delhi.

——(1986) National Policy on Education, 1986, Government of India, New Delhi.

——(1992) National Policy on Education, 1986 (Revised 1992), Government of India, New Delhi.

Mukherjee, R. (2008) Towards Legitimate Role for Foreign Institutions, *Seminar* July.

Musgrave, R. A. (1959) *Theory of Public Finance*, McGraw Hill, New York.

Naik, J.P. (1982) *Education Commission and After*, Allied Publishers Private Limited, New Delhi.

Narayana, M.R. (2006) Privatization Policies and Post Privatization control devices in India's Higher Education: Evidence from a Regional Study and Implications for Developing Countries, *Journal of Studies in International Education*, vol. 10 (1), spring, pp. 46-70.

Oza, N. (1999) System of Higher Education: Emerging Scenario, in Oza, N. and Joshi, K.M. (1999) (ed.) *Privatization of Education: Issues and Options*, Mangal Deep Publications, Jaipur.

Parmaji (1985); *Caste Reservations and Performance: Research Findings*, Warangal, AP: Mamta Publications.

Patel, S. (2004) Higher Education at the Crossroads, *Economic and Political Weekly* (Special articles) 22nd May.

Patwardhan, V. and Palshikar, V. (1992) Reserved Seats in Medical Education: A Study, *Journal of Education and Social Change*, 5:1.

Periyasamy, P. (2004) Globalization of Higher Education: Means for India, *University News*, 4-10 October.

Pinto, A. (2000) Globalization and the Changing Ideology of Indian Higher Education, *Social Action*, vol. 50, Oct.-Dec. pp. 333-347.

Powar, K.B. (2002) *Internationalization of Higher Education*, New Delhi: Association of Indian Universities, New Delhi.

Prajapati, G.K. (1982) Impact of Education on Social, Economic and Political Changes Among Scheduled Castes: A Case Study of Danapur sub Division, 1982, In Third Survey of Research in Education.

Prakash, V. (2007) Higher Education in India- Growth and the Diversity of Expectations, *International Review of Education*, France, September.

Prakash, V. (2008) 'Education, Equality and Social Justice: An Indian Scenario, Paper presented in the 2nd International Symposium and Public forum on "Education, Equality and Social Justice" organized in Brasilia and Campo Grande from April 24.

Prasad, J. S. (2002) Changing Role of Higher Education in India with Special Reference to Liberalization, M. Phil. Dissertation, New Delhi, Jawaharlal Nehru University.

Premi, K. K. (1983) Trends of Enrollment of the Scheduled Caste Students in Higher Education (1964-77), National Institute of Educational Planning and Administration, New Delhi.

Premsai, C. (NA) Higher Education in India: From Socialism to Capitalism, http://www.legalserviceindia.com/articles/he.htm.

Psacharapoulos, G.P. and Patrinos, A.H. (2002) Returns to Investment in Education: A Further Update, World Bank Policy Research Working Paper, 2881 In Chalam, K.S. (2007) Privatization of Higher Education Under WTO Regime, *University News* 42(07).

Psarcharopoulos, G. (1994) Returns to Investment in Education: A Global Update, *World Development*, 22(9), pp. 1325-43.

Rao, S. S. (2001) *Equality in Higher Education: Impact of Affirmative Action Policies in India.* Unpublished Draft Paper. New Delhi: JNU.

Reddy S. B. (2001) Attitudes of Scheduled Caste University Students Towards Reservation And Its Implication, *Indian Anthropologist*, vol. 31:1, p. 29-43.

Report of Commissioner of Scheduled Caste and Scheduled Tribes (1978-79), 26th Report.

Report of National Knowledge Commission on Higher Education (2006).

Sachidananda and Sinha, Ramesh P. (1989) *Education and the Disadvantaged*, Uppal Publishing House, New Delhi.

Sadlak J. (1998) Globalization and Concurrent Challenges for Higher Education, in Scott, P. (1998) (ed.) *The Globalization of Higher Education*. The society for Research into Higher Education and Open University Press, Bury St. Edmunds.

Sarkar, S. (1983) *Modern India 1885-1947*, MacMillan Publishers, Delhi-2

Scott, P. (1998) Massification, Internationalization and Globalization, in Scott, P. (1998) (ed.) *The Globalization of Higher Education*. The society for Research into Higher Education and Open University Press, Bury St. Edmunds.

Sewell, W. H. (1971) Inequalityof Opportunity for Higher Education. *American Sociological Review*. Vol. 36, No. 5, pp. 793-809.

Sharma, G.D. (1989) Alternative policy of Financing Education: An analysis in the political Economy of Financing, (Singh and Sharma) (ed.) *Higher Education in India- The Social Context*, Konark Publishers, New Delhi.

Sharma, G.D. (2000) Financing of Higher Education in India: in Retrospects and Prospects, in Policy Recommendations of Financing for Higher Education: A Report of Consultative Committee Meeting, NIEPA, New Delhi.

Sharma, K.L (1974) Educational Inequalities Among Rajasthan Scheduled Castes, *Economic and Political Weekly*, 14 Sep. vol. ix (37).

Sharma, V. (2007) Privatization of Higher Education is the Main aim, *People's Democracy*, vol. xxxi no. 7 Feb.18.

Singh, P. (1989) *Problem of Education Among Scheduled Castes*, Mittal Publications, New Delhi.

Singh, R. (2005) Privatization of Higher Education in the Era of Globalization, *University News,* 43 (34) p. 13.

Sinha, S. and Sinha, P. R. (1989) *Education and the Disadvantaged,* New Delhi: Uppal Publication House.

Sinha, S. (1977) *The Harijan Elite*, Thomson Press, New Delhi.

Sinha, S. (2009) *Equity and Access to Higher Education in India*, Unpublished Paper. New Delhi: JNU.

Srivastava, R. (2008) Regulating the Private Sector, *Seminar*, July.

Sundaram, K. (2007) *Fair Access to Higher Education Revisited: Some Results for Social and Religious Groups from NSS 61st Round Employment Unemployment Survey 2004-05,* Working paper no. 163. Centre for development economics. New Delhi: Delhi School of Economics.

Teltumbde, A. (2007) State, Market and Dalits, *Indian Journal Of Social Work*, 1 January, pp. 34-55.

Teltumbde, A. (2008) State, Market, and Development of Dalits, *Social Action*, vol. 58, January-March.

Teltumbde, A. (NA) Globalization and the Dalits, http://ambedkar.org/research/globalisationandthedalits.pdf.

Thorat S. (2005) Why Reservation is Necessary? *Seminar*, Vol. 549, May-2005.

Thorat, S. (2006) Higher Education in India, Emerging Issues Related to Access, Inclusiveness and Quality, Nehru Memorial Lecture, University of Mumbai, Mumbai.

Thorat, S. (2009) OP-ED Article from *The Asian Age* Newspaper, 14th March 2009.

Tilak, J.B.G. (1991) The Privatization of Higher Education, *Prospects* vol. xxi, no. 2, 1991, pp. 229-239.

Tilak, J.B.G. (1997) Five Decades of Underinvestment in Education, *Economic and Political Weekly*, Sep. 6, pp. 2239-2241.

Tilak, J.B.G. (1997) Lessons from Cost Recovery in Education, In Oxford Colctough (ed.) Marketing Education and Health in Developing Countries: Miracle or Mirage?, Clarendon Press, pp. 63-89.

Tilak, J.B.G. (1999) Privatization of Higher Education, *Prospects*, vol. 21, no. 2.

Tilak, J.B.G. (2004) Absence of Policy and Perspective in Higher Education, *Economic and Political Weekly,* May 22: 2159-2164.

Tilak, J.B.G. (2005) Are we Marching Towards Laissez- Faireism in Higher Education Development?, *Journal of International Cooperation in Education.* vol. 8(1), pp. 151-165.

Tinto, V. (1975) Dropout from Higher Education: A Theoretical Synthesis of Recent Research, *Review of Educational Research*, vol. 45, no. 1 (winter), pp. 89-125.

Tinto, V. (1982) Limits of Theory and Practice in Student Attrition, *The Journal of Higher Education*, vol. 53, no. 6, pp. 687-700.

Tooley, M and Dixon, P. (2006) Defacto Privatization of education and the Poor: Implications of a study from Sub-Saharan Africa and India', *Compare*, vol. 36, no. 4, Dec., pp. 443-462.

University Grants Commission (1992) *UGC Funding of Institutions of Higher Education.* Report of Justice K. Punnayya Committee. New Delhi.

Velaskar, P. (1986) *Inequality in Higher Education: A Study of Scheduled Caste Students in Medical Colleges of Bombay.* Unpublished Ph.D. Thesis. Bombay: TISS.

Verghese, N.V. (2001) Higher Education and Distributional Equity, *Perspectives in Education*, vol. 17-special issue, pp. 95-108.

Waghmore, S. (2008) Exploring the Unexplored- Dalit Worldview in Development Discourse, *Social Action*, vol. 58, Jan.-March, pp. 17-23.

Walford, J. and Kaul, R. (1990) Privatization and Privilege in Education, Ruotledge publications, London in Aggarwal, Vidya and Sharma, R.U. (2004) Privatization vs Commercialization of Higher Education: Some Facts, Concerns and Suggestions, *University News* 42(7), pp. 25-28.

Wankhede, G.G. (2003) The Scheduled Castes and Higher Education in India-Retrospects and Prospects, *Think India Quarterly,* vol. 6 (3) pp. 29-39.

Weisskopf, T. E. (2004) Impact of Reservation on Admissions to Higher Education in India, *Economic and Political Weekly*, 25 September, pp. 4339-4349.

Web Address: http://aka.lawstudent.in/bc_seervai_essay.htm